Healing After Divorce

Healing After Divorce

Healing After Divorce

(Second Edition)

Grace, Mercy and Remarriage

Bill Vincent

Revival Waves of Glory Books & Publishing has allowed this work to remain exactly as the author intended, verbatim, without editorial input.

All Scripture quotations are from the Authorized King James Version of the Bible unless otherwise noted.

Softcover: 978-0692648681

PUBLISHED BY REVIVAL WAVES OF GLORY BOOKS & PUBLISHING
www.revivalwavesofgloryministries.com
Litchfield, IL

Published in the United States of America

Table of Contents

Dedication

I dedicate this book to my Wife Tabitha and our new Baby Arianna Grace Vincent. If it wasn't for the healing power of God of past relationships my Wife and I would not have experienced the joy of this beautiful girl. I love you Arianna and I love you Tabitha my first real love.

Introduction

This book is being released because God has been urging me for a long time to release healing through this book. Divorce is considered to be unforgivable to many Christian beliefs. For many months this book has been in the process. This book is for more than the divorced person but also those who want to find God's heart concerning the topics of divorce and remarriage. Before we get started I want you to know it is true that God HATES divorce and we should never jump at the first opportunity to divorce the one we once loved. There is a lot that we are going to get into so may you receive revelation for yourself and let it set you free as you read LIFE AFTER DIVORCE.

What does the Bible and God really say about divorce and remarriage. God doesn't want us bound by the false traditions of men, so this book gives specifics to help anyone looking for answers. The restoration of troubled marriages is still God's first priority. We also will see Biblical answers given on how we can, with the help of the Lord, overcome the negative emotions of grief, anger, depression, bitterness, unforgiveness, and rejection, so we can live the happy, fruitful, and abundant lives that God desires for all of his children!

CHAPTER ONE
The Church's Position

This topic of the Church's Position is what this whole book was originally written for. I Want to help to give you a clear picture of some things to understand in your healing process. There are thousands of Christians who struggle with the issue of divorce on a daily basis. They receive different and often conflicting information from their friends and even their pastors and their churches. In the midst of their emotional pain and confusion, they find themselves wrestling with possible intellectual confusion as well. If you fit into this category, I want to assure you that you are not alone. In this chapter we will examine the Church's position. There are principles of interpretation of Scripture, that I want to lay out before we start, as I think that they are important to the proper understanding of Scripture. We must not be closed minded as God brings fresh insight of His Word.

First, Scripture should be examined through the eyes of the people to whom it was addressed. This takes into account both their language and their culture. Think about the changes that have occurred even in our short lifetime. This same concept is true for things written thousands of years before us. The teachings of the Scriptures should be viewed in relation to the culture for which they were written. Because certain concepts are already understood in a particular culture, the Scriptures may not mention a key point because it would be unneeded. Scripture is not so complicated that only the local intellects are able to understand it. The basic meaning of Scripture is the clear understanding that an ordinary person would have in the culture in which it was written.

In the Garden of Eden, we see God's clear and simple design for marriage.

Genesis 2:24 Therefore shall a man leave his father and his mother, and shall cleave unto his wife: and they shall be one flesh.

Two individuals come together and become one. That's the deal. And it worked great until someone didn't like something that his or her spouse did, something that was said, a repeatedly annoying behavior, and so on. Then people began to look for a way out of being one flesh. One thing I want you to understand is that the primary meaning of covenant during this time was an agreement between two parties that was mutually binding. As a part of this covenant or contract, money was exchanged. The groom made payments for the bride, and the bride's father would give an offering, which was often viewed as her portion of her father's inheritance. All of this was a part of sealing the deal from a contractual view point. By the time of Moses, things had become messy. During that time, with rare exceptions, men had the right to divorce their wives. Understand that God never instituted divorce. But once the people began to practice it, and abuse the reputations of women, God allowed Moses to give the people instructions. It had become all too common for a man to become displeased with his wife and then send her away. If the woman was sent away, people believed it was because she had been unfaithful or indecent. If a woman was sent away, unfaithful or not, her reputation was ruined. By the time of Moses it had become necessary for God to provide rules on the actions to be followed in situations where divorce occurs, because men were now practicing marriage destruction. Evidently some were doing so, in cruel and heartless ways by putting their wives out without giving them a full legal release. The woman was not permitted by law to marry another husband. Being virtually without personal legal rights, she was ruined. Many women in that situation turned to prostitution as a means of survival. So God gave instruction through Moses that in the case where a man had decided to put away his wife he must give her a written certificate or bill of divorce.

Deuteronomy 24:1 When a man hath taken a wife, and married her, and it come to pass that she find no favour in his eyes, because he hath found some uncleanness in her: then **let him write her a bill of divorcement, and give *it* in her hand, and send her out of his house.**

The husband had no further claim on her, could not demand that she return, and could not dishonor her reputation by saying that she had left by her own choice. Once the woman had been given this certificate, she was free to remarry. The only limitation was that she could not marry her lover or the person with whom she was suspected of committing adultery, if this had in fact been the issue of divorce. While we find Moses' instructions for how to handle divorce, we have to remember that God despised what men and women were doing to each other. By the end of the Old Testament, unfaithfulness was out of control, and not just in marriages. People had made unfaithfulness to God, and each other, a way of life. God is more than crystal clear when He spoke through the prophet Malachi.

Malachi 2:16 "For I hate divorce," says the LORD, the God of Israel, "and him who covers his garment with wrong," says the LORD of hosts. "So take heed to your spirit, that you do not deal treacherously." (NAM)

Malachi 2:16 For the LORD, the God of Israel, saith that he hateth putting away: for *one* covereth violence with his garment, saith the LORD of hosts: therefore take heed to your spirit, that ye deal not treacherously. (KJV)

He hates the unfaithfulness in marriages. Malachi even implies that, when we break the covenant with our spouse, God will no longer pay attention to our offering.

After a closer look at scripture the law of marriage changed drastically. Men and women were both able to divorce at will and needed no grounds to do so. A woman would lose her offering if she was divorced for adultery and a man would have to return the offering plus a half if he committed adultery, but divorce for other grounds was without any penalty. All of this contributed to a great deal of instability within the institution of marriage.

Based on a passage in Exodus 21 regarding obligations in marriage, the rabbis during the time of Jesus generally believed that the following were appropriate grounds for divorce: childlessness, material neglect, emotional neglect, and unfaithfulness. Following what would have been considered a valid divorce, remarriage was generally accepted. If it took place following an invalid divorce, it was considered adultery.

Josephus acknowledged that the sole purpose for a marriage was to procreate. Based upon this premise, infertility was therefore considered by some to be a ground for divorce. Any couple who did not have children within ten years of marriage was expected to divorce. Each party was to remarry someone with whom they might be fertile. However, there were rabbis who argued against this practice. The stain of adultery continued in the New Testament. While a person could marry a divorcee or widow, if the woman had been divorced because of adultery, the couple often faced a great shame. There were two primary thoughts regarding the matter of divorce, and these adopted quite opposite views. As you might expect, this led to great controversy, debate, and, of course, confusion and uncertainty. The two positions were developed primarily from different interpretations of one passage of Scripture, in particular.

Deuteronomy 24:1 When a man hath taken a wife, and married her, and **it come to pass that she find no favour in his eyes, because he hath found some uncleanness in her:** then let him write her a bill of divorcement, and give *it* in her hand, and send her out of his house.

The instructions continue on from there. The two words that have formed the basis for this controversy are some uncleaness.

Jesus walked onto this stage of debate in Matthew 19 when the Pharisees came to ask Him about this matter. They wanted to know if it was all right for married couples to divorce using the any reason argument. Jesus' response was a resounding, NO! I want you to notice here that Jesus didn't buy into the rabbinical debate. He was making God's position from the beginning clear, as I quoted from Genesis earlier. He acknowledged that Moses allowed divorce because of people's hard, stubborn hearts but that God's plan was that two people should remain together. He allows for divorce in the case of adultery, but it is interesting to note that even then, it is not commanded but allowed. It would almost appear to imply that the innocent party could forgive the offending spouse and should perhaps only invoke this exception if the guilty party continues his or her sinful pattern, refusing to repent of that lifestyle and embrace one of faithfulness. Much has been written regarding the idea that if a man divorces his wife for a reason other than unfaithfulness.

Matthew 5:32 But I say unto you, That whosoever shall put away his wife, saving for the cause of fornication, causeth her to commit adultery: and whosoever shall marry her that is divorced committeth adultery.

It is possible that Jesus was talking about how people will perceive this woman and her new husband. By divorcing his wife for any reason, he is victimizing her. Others will assume and believe the worst possible thing about this woman and may even suspect that her new husband was her lover, and consequently the reason for the divorce. While these facts would be in error, the perception would remain. The apostle Paul gives us additional thoughts on divorce and remarriage when he writes his first letter to the Corinthians.

1 Corinthians 7:10, 11 And unto the married I command, *yet* not I, but the Lord, Let not the wife depart from *her* husband: But and if she depart, let her remain unmarried, or be reconciled to *her* husband: and let not the husband put away *his* wife.

At first glance, it would appear that Paul is making a distinction between a separation and a divorce. However, this difference will disappear when one realizes that in the time that, both men and women could divorce their partner by separation. It was considered a legal divorce. As a matter of fact, if Paul were only talking about separation, then stating that she should not remarry wouldn't make any sense, because she would still be married. She could not be referred to as unmarried. However, since the separation is actually a divorce, then she would be unmarried. Paul was writing into this context. If divorce happened by this method, it was important that believers did all that they could to turn it around.

Paul continued on in this passage by addressing the issue of remarriage. He stated that when a believer is divorced by a nonbeliever against his will, the believer is not bound in this situation. Paul declared "God has called us in peace." The practical solution that he proposed is that all those who have been divorced against their will, and who therefore can do nothing to reverse it should be regarded as genuinely divorced; they are no longer bound by their marriage contract and are free to remarry. What if I was divorced by a believer?" I have found many interesting and diverse thoughts regarding this issue. Some would say that the believer is stuck and cannot remarry. Martin Luther "implied that a believer who deserted his or her spouse was worse than an unbeliever."

Others continue reasoning when they examine the model of discipline that the Church is to follow as discussed in Matthew

18. In this model, the believer who leaves should be privately asked by his or her spouse to return. If he or she refuses, then the spouse is to take a witness with them and make the request again. If the believer still refuses, then he or she is to be taken before the Church and again asked to return. Should the person continue to refuse, he or she is to be withdrawn from Church membership and regarded as an unbeliever. If believers are deserted by believing partners, Paul commands the deserters to return. There appears to be no doubt that the believers will obey this command. Paul does not even discuss the possibility that believing deserters will not return to their partners. If believers did refuse to obey this command, and thereby refuse to obey the direct command of Jesus, the Church would presumably be forced to excommunicate them. While this line of reasoning may seem harsh in the 21st century, I wonder if that is partly because we have become afraid of hurting people's feelings and don't want to offend. Church discipline has become a teaching that resides that the Church doesn't hear any more. We need true teaching with pure discipline. Even the Church has occasionally been guilty of adopting a live-and-let-live policy. Yet, Jesus was very clear about the manner in which the Church should respond to blatant disobedience. Many believe that Jesus referred specifically to adultery and that Paul's allowance for desertion is a reference to the lack of material and emotional support mentioned in Exodus 21. Regarding remarriage, it has been observed that, The New Testament teaching on remarriage after a valid divorce, is admittedly, ambiguous and unclear. However, remarriage after divorce was a fundamental right in the first-century world and it was often regarded as an obligation. The New Testament writers knew that they would have to articulate their teaching extremely clear and unmistakably if they wanted to teach the opposite of this universally held view.

I have come to understand the teachings of the New Testament, I would sum up them as follows. The Jewish culture held two different positions: divorce for adultery only or divorce for "any reason." Jesus addressed these arguments when He said that couples are not to divorce for any reason. He clearly stated that from the beginning, God designed a man and a woman to marry, be united, and become one flesh. Once they are married, God has joined them together, and they are to never be separated! However, if one of the individuals practices a lifestyle of unrepentant continued adultery, then a divorce is allowed. Yet, God's desire is still love, forgiveness, and reconciliation. Paul continued on by saying that couples are not to divorce. If a couple does divorce, they are to either reconcile their marriage or remain single. However, if the believer's spouse, either a nonbeliever or a believer who refuses to obey Jesus and the discipline of the Church, deserts them, then they are no longer bound and are free to remarry. Yet, while there seem to be clearly allowed grounds for divorce, I again emphasize that God's desire is not for us to waste our energy looking for loopholes and reasons to get a divorce. The Holy Spirit's continued conviction is that we intently look for ways to fix, heal, love, forgive, reconcile, restore, and unite our marriage for the remainder of our lives. That, and nothing less, is the focus taught in the New Testament.

Before I go on, I want to note that God does forgive all sins that we sin through repentance. The only sin we can't be forgiven according to Scripture is blaspheme of the Holy Spirit.

The Catholic Church adopted a position that a true marriage was a religious sacrament that could not be dissolved by legal means. Their view is that divorces are merely a form of legal separation, and remarriage is not permitted. This view in the Catholic Church has continued into the present. One way they have been able to allow some divorces is to say that they weren't a true marriage. They are able to make this distinction, for example, based upon whether the marriage was performed in the Catholic Church. If it was, the marriage cannot be ended in the eyes of the Church. However, if the marriage was performed in a Protestant Church, by a justice of the peace, or by another means, the Catholic Church may not consider that to be a valid marriage and can grant an annulment. The individuals can then remarry, since they were never really married according to Catholic doctrine.

Another look into a belief is that Divorce, in the sense of a formal, legal pronouncement that a marriage was terminated, always meant the end of that marriage, whether it was done for right reasons or wrong reasons. The notion that a marriage broken for wrong reasons somehow continues to live on in the eyes of God, after formal divorce, is entirely an invention of man and has no basis in Scripture. The explicit statement of God himself is that after the written divorce is given she may go and be another man's wife. Never in any culture has the divorce decree meant that a marriage remains intact in anyone's eyes. Neither has it ever meant release for one party from the marriage bond but not the other. All such nonsense came on the scene much later, long after the end of divine revelation and the completion of the Bible. It grew out of great confusion in a period we generally call the dark ages. As you can see, the understanding of what is Biblically allowed and what isn't didn't become clearer with time, but only more confusing. Even during the 20th century, we have seen a similar swinging of the doctrine, just in different ways. During the first half of the century, there was a condescending attitude toward those who were divorced. They were often viewed as second-class citizens in the Church. Even if an individual was perceived as a victim, they were still viewed through a filter or stigma of suspicion and were not seen as equal to those who were not divorced. People would question, Can the divorced individual serve? Can they teach Sunday school, sing in the choir, or serve as an elder or deacon? Some were concerned that if divorcees were allowed to serve, others would see this as an endorsement of divorce. The danger is that divorce would become an outbreak. The Church began to offer more grace and understanding. They began to minister to the needs of those hurting because of divorce and examined the specific needs of single parents. Certainly, the Church's position needs to change. The Church needs to demonstrate grace and see divorcees through God's eyes. Yet, in doing so, the Church began to stop addressing the sin of divorce. Suddenly, the Church took a hands-off approach. The leadership didn't want to ask too many questions lest they be seen as judgmental. In other words, love that is a sham. You see, true love is willing to love in the hard times, speak truth, set boundaries, and hold others accountable. But this blanketed unquestioning acceptance was nothing of the sort. Yet, in the world's eyes, questions and accountability indicated rigid rules and a judgmental attitude. Certainly Christians didn't want to be accused of that, so we jumped on the everything is OK. Christians began to throw everything under the only God can judge bus, absolving those at fault of all responsibility. It sounds progressively good. The only problem is, this is contrary to the teachings of Jesus, the apostles, and even the Old Testament writers. What a wide swing in a short few decades.

So I am going to continue to look at a number of things so you don't have to just take my word for it. You have to get your own revelation of God's goodness and love through healing and restoration of repentance.

CHAPTER TWO
Practices in the Church

As we look further into the Church's practices. This is to help us understand where the Church stands concerning divorce. In order to get as accurate a perspective as possible regarding current practices, I have approached this in an objective, worldwide manner as well as in a local, experiential one. I wanted to know what churches are doing across the country. How are they approaching divorcees and their needs? What does their ministry to singles look like? How do they handle moral issues? What is their position on remarriage? Are they doing anything to address divorce prevention and marriage restoration? The results were wide in range and presented a good picture of what is taking place in our churches.

While I am encouraged by the position that the Church has taken in recent years to minister to those recovering from the devastation of divorce, I am particularly interested in its approach to those who are still married.

Some churches adopt a very hands-off process that concerns me. The Church has the opportunity to bring life, hope, and wisdom into the process. If we fail to do that, I wonder if we are not guilty of what Jesus would refer to as the salt losing its saltiness. He says that when that happens,

Matthew 5:13 Ye are the salt of the earth: but if the salt have lost his savour, wherewith shall it be salted? it is thenceforth good for nothing, but to be cast out, and to be trodden under foot of men.

At many points in history, aspects of the Church have unfortunately fit that description. The Church has the opportunity to intervene and be the light of the world that it was created to be. It is important that we not renounce that role; if we do, we have ceased to be the body God has called us to be.

Some churches have watched their singles die a slow death. Others have been able to develop thriving ministries. I don't really like the singles events in Church. Churches host activities like Bible studies, football and basketball leagues, hiking, Christian concerts, bowling, movies, Sunday school, Saturday night socials, Tuesday night dinners, coffeehouse discussions about relevant topics, dance lessons, Sunday brunches, retreats, and worship teams. single moms in the church and singles dating. I'm a firm believer that God is the one that puts people together. The thing that needs to be in Churches is help to the divorced families.

Obviously many churches have developed programs for hurting individuals following the marriage train wreck. It is terrific that we have developed programs to meet the needs of people where they are. However, with the divorce rate in the Church reflecting that of the world, I was interested in what we are doing, not just reactively after the disaster, but proactively to prevent the disaster. By the divorce rate, it is clear that we have not done a very good job in this area. Some of the various programs offered included: classes on making marriages stronger; marriage retreats; Bible studies for married couples. It is encouraging to see how seriously many churches have taken this matter and the efforts they are making to address this vital problem and need. At the same time, the fact that a huge percent of churches are not tackling these difficult issues is disturbing.

A small amount of Churches today have no objections to the subject of remarriage. All kinds of decisions are made where this is concerned which I discussed in Chapter One.

Because marriage has been established by God as an indissoluble union, and since it is an earthly copy of the relationship between God and his people, it is to be kept inviolate. However, because of the fallen-ness of human nature, the Scriptures permit divorce in the following cases as disdain to human frailty for the protection of the innocent party:

1. Divorce for the cause of immorality with the understanding that the obligation to maintain or reinstate the marriage may not be imposed upon the innocent spouse.

2. Divorce for desertion-desertion being defined as behavior equivalent to the abandonment of the marriage relationship. In such cases, the offending party becomes subject to church discipline in order to bring about repentance and reconciliation. Should efforts to achieve restoration fail, the innocent spouse is not bound. He or she becomes free to remarry in the Lord.

The remarriage of believers may not be approved when:

1. Divorce is being used as a vehicle to seek a different mate, since such pre-intent makes the divorce adulterous.

2. There is no evidence of repentance and brokenness over the circumstances that caused the divorce.

3. Restoration of the original marriage remains a viable option. Each case of divorce or remarriage has to be dealt with on an individual basis from the perspective of God's inexhaustible capacity to forgive human sin and restore broken lives.

Matthew 18:15 Moreover if thy brother shall trespass against thee, go and tell him his fault between thee and him alone: if he shall hear thee, thou hast gained thy brother.

Chapter Three Recovery from Divorce

Some of the things I've learned from dealing with this and seeking the Lord are in this book. But here I want to take a look at growing, healing, understanding your identity, forgiveness, letting go of the past and finally taking on new responsibilities.

Some other powerful topics we will examine is moving toward acceptance, coping with loss, understanding emotions, growing, dangers to avoid, healing wounds and feeling good about yourself.

Most marriages start out with both parties bringing some problems into the marriage. This is the result of hurts of childhood or even previous relationships that have caused us to live life with painful things. These things I'm talking about are what the enemy loves to stir up.

After someone experiences divorce there is a need that must be met. Figuring out who you are as a single person, grieving your loss, letting go, learning to forgive, and growing into a strong and healthy individual who can stand and be okay by him or herself are all common threads that needs to be emphasized. I want you to know that Pain is inevitable, but misery is an option.

The Church is doing a better job today of ministering to and validating those who have weathered divorce. However, we are still weak when it comes to our willingness to take a more active role in restoration and prevention. Clearly, in the area of reconciliation and restoration, the Church has demonstrated timidity. Only some have really been willing to get in the trenches and do what needs to be done to encourage the saving and healing of marriages. All of the Church needs to rise up and be the Church that God has called us to be in a world that is chaotically lost and spiraling out of control. The world should not be the champion of marriage and the family. If the Church doesn't fill that void, then no one will. If marriage, as God designed it, is not to become a thing of the past, the Church must rise up and fulfill her role.

It can be a painful journey, and I invite you to come with me down a path that I believe will help provide some support, encouragement, reassurances, and solid biblical answers for the questions and situations you face. And most importantly, I hope you will discover that God does truly understand and He cares.

The question most people want answered is what is God's will on remarriage.

"God hates divorce" (Malachi 2:16).

The pain, confusion, and frustration most people experience after a divorce are surely part of the reason that God hates divorce. Even more difficult, biblically, than the question of divorce, is the question of remarriage. The vast majority of people who divorce either remarry or consider getting remarried. What does the Bible say about this?

Matthew 19:9 And I say unto you, Whosoever shall put away his wife, except *it be* for fornication, and shall marry another, committeth adultery: and whoso marrieth her which is put away doth commit adultery.

Matthew 5:32 But I say unto you, That whosoever shall put away his wife, saving for the cause of fornication, causeth her to commit adultery: and whosoever shall marry her that is divorced committeth adultery.

What does the Bible say about divorce and remarriage? Plain and simple question of "I am divorced. Can I remarry?"

It is my view that there are certain instances in which divorce and remarriage are permitted without the remarriage being considered adultery. These instances would include unrepentant adultery, physical abuse of spouse or children, and abandonment of a believing spouse by an unbelieving spouse. I am not saying that a person under such circumstances should remarry.

1 Corinthians 7:11 But and if she depart, let her remain unmarried, or be reconciled to *her* husband: and let not the husband put away *his* wife.

The Bible encourages reconciliation before remarriage. At the same time, it is my view that God offers His mercy and grace to the innocent party in a divorce and allows that person to remarry without it being considered adultery. This can also be considered if the spouse is demonic to the point of no return in such a case of a Jezebel Spirit.

The scriptures I'm listing are what many use to back up the idea that remarriage is never a option.

Luke 16:18 Whosoever putteth away his wife, and marrieth another, committeth adultery: and whosoever marrieth her that is put away from *her* husband committeth adultery.

The question then becomes, is this remarriage an act of adultery, or a state of adultery. Here are some scripture that show adultery in the present tense.

Matthew 5:32 But I say unto you, That whosoever shall put away his wife, saving for the cause of fornication, causeth her to commit adultery: and whosoever shall marry her that is divorced committeth adultery.

Matthew 19:9 And I say unto you, Whosoever shall put away his wife, except *it be* for fornication, and shall marry another, committeth adultery: and whoso marrieth her which is put away doth commit adultery.

Luke 16:18 Shows a continuous state of adultery.

Luke 16:18 Whosoever putteth away his wife, and marrieth another, committeth adultery: and whosoever marrieth her that is put away from *her* husband committeth adultery.

At the same time, the present tense in Greek does not always indicate continuous action. Sometimes it simply means that something occurred. For example, the word "divorces" in Matthew 5:32 is present tense, but divorcing is not a continual action. It is my view that remarriage, no matter the circumstances, is not a continual state of adultery. Only the act of getting remarried itself is adultery. According to Scripture is all we have to go by. Before I go deeper into this here is a big thought, "If a man even lusts in his heart he has committed adultery." We do have a God whom forgives us despite our past sins. If some has been married more than once and then gets saved do they have to leave their current husband to be right in the eyes of God. I know I'm stirring you because of the dancing around my belief but that is the only way you and I get revelation. We have to get all the info and lay it out to make it plain.

Now lets look at some in the Old Testament Law, the punishment for adultery was death.

Leviticus 20:10 And the man that committeth adultery with *another* man's wife, *even he* that committeth adultery with his neighbour's wife, the adulterer and the adulteress shall surely be put to death.

Deuteronomy 24:1-4 When a man hath taken a wife, and married her, and it come to pass that she find no favour in his eyes, because he hath found some uncleanness in her: then let him write her a bill of divorcement, and give *it* in her hand, and send her out of his house. And when she is departed out of his house, she may go and be another man's *wife*. And *if* the latter husband hate her, and write her a bill of divorcement, and giveth *it* in her hand, and sendeth her out of his house; or if the latter husband die, which took her *to be* his wife; Her former husband, which sent her away, may not take her again to be his wife, after that she is defiled; for that *is* abomination before the LORD: and thou shalt not cause the land to sin, which the LORD thy God giveth thee *for* an inheritance.

This mentions remarriage after a divorce and does not call it adultery and does not demand the death penalty for the remarried spouse.

The Bible clearly says that God hates divorce (Malachi 2:16), but nowhere explicitly states that God hates remarriage. The Bible nowhere commands a remarried couple to divorce. Deuteronomy 24 does not describe the remarriage as invalid. Ending a remarriage through divorce would be just as sinful as ending a first marriage through divorce. Both would include the breaking of vows before God, between the couple, and in front of witnesses.

It doesn't matter the circumstances, once a couple is remarried, they should strive to live out their married lives in faithfulness, in a God-honoring way, with Christ at the center of their marriage. A marriage is a marriage. God does not view the new marriage as invalid or adulterous. A remarried couple should devote themselves to God, and to each other and honor Him by making their new marriage a lasting and Christ-centered one.

Ephesians 5:22, 23 Wives, submit yourselves unto your own husbands, as unto the Lord. For the husband is the head of the wife, even as Christ is the head of the church: and he is the saviour of the body.

Ephesians 5:25 Husbands, love your wives, even as Christ also loved the church, and gave himself for it;

More on this wonderful topic of remarriage and divorce. Lets look at it different ways again. In a general sense, God allows only three reasons for the dissolution of a marriage. The first reason is obvious death of one of the individuals in the marriage.

Romans 7:2 For the woman which hath an husband is bound by the law to *her* husband so long as he liveth; but if the husband be dead, she is loosed from the law of *her* husband.

The second reason is adultery or immorality on the part of one of the individuals.

Matthew 5:31, 32 It hath been said, Whosoever shall put away his wife, let him give her a writing of divorcement: But I say unto you, That whosoever shall put away his wife, saving for the cause of fornication, causeth her to commit adultery: and whosoever shall marry her that is divorced committeth adultery.

Matthew 19:9 And I say unto you, Whosoever shall put away his wife, except *it be* for fornication, and shall marry another, committeth adultery: and whoso marrieth her which is put away doth commit adultery.

1 Corinthians 7:12-16 But to the rest speak **I, not the Lord**: If any brother hath a wife that believeth not, and she be pleased to dwell with him, let him not put her away. And the woman which hath an husband that believeth not, and if he be pleased to dwell with her, let her not leave him. For the unbelieving husband is sanctified by the wife, and the unbelieving wife is sanctified by the husband: else were your children unclean; but now are they holy. But if the unbelieving depart, let him depart. A brother or a sister is not under bondage in such *cases:* but God hath called us to peace. For what knowest thou, O wife, whether thou shalt save *thy* husband? or how knowest thou, O man, whether thou shalt save *thy* wife?

Look at this when Paul wrote “I, not the Lord” in that passage, he did not say that this was not from God, but rather that Jesus had never addressed this topic Himself. Here Paul states that "if the unbeliever departs" the Christian is not under bondage. The same concept is used again.

1 Corinthians 7:39 The wife is bound by the law as long as her husband liveth; but if her husband be dead, she is at liberty to be married to whom she will; only in the Lord.

As a rule you allow the author to define the terms by what is stated in other areas of the same document. This is the author's intended meaning. A Christian is not bound to their marriage if the unbeliever leaves them. In each of these cases, it seems that God is trying to protect the innocent party that is left to live their life after the marriage ends. Please understand that this is a brief writing of this subject.

Now let's look at a situation that does not include one of these acceptable divorces. Many people do believe that remarriage after such a divorce constitutes continuous adultery that cannot be repented of (if you remain in the marriage). They would say that these people should divorce again and either be reunited to their original spouse or remain single.

Romans 7:3 So then if, while *her* husband liveth, she be married to another man, she shall be called an adulteress: but if her husband be dead, she is free from that law; so that she is no adulteress, though she be married to another man.

It is a possible position to take. Still, remarriage to the same spouse after being married to someone else in between violates Deuteronomy 24:4. It is important to note that Romans 7:3 was not designed by Paul to be the end rule statement of divorce and remarriage, it was actually using marriage in general to illustrate a point about the Law. Obviously God did provide for marriage to end in two other ways besides death. This is not to say that God is soft on divorce. Jesus said that it was only because of our hardness of heart that God allowed divorce.

Matthew 19:8 He saith unto them, Moses because of the **hardness of your hearts** suffered you to put away your wives: but from the beginning it was not so.

Ezra chapters 9 and 10 are sometimes used to support getting a divorce to obey God. However, the reason for divorce in these chapters was to keep the Jewish people pure for the Messiah to come through their lineage. They had intermarried with those other than Jews, which was in direct violation of God's commandment to them. The situation was very different from our situation today. Malachi 2:16 says that God hates divorce, and we think everyone knows that divorce is wrong before God.

The issue many have probably decided to read this book is in the Sub-title. That is the topic of remarriage. The real issue that people wonder about is remarriage. Although God has not given specific information regarding the acceptability of remarriage, I can give you some things to think about in this area.

2 Corinthians 5:17 Therefore if any man *be* in Christ, *he is* a new creature: old things are passed away; behold, all

things are become new.

Obviously, based on 2 Corinthians 5:17, if someone has had a failed marriage, and *later* got right with God, "all things are become new" you get a clean slate as though you had not been divorced.

Romans 8:28 And we know that all things work together for good to them that love God, to them who are the called according to *his* purpose.

God can use bad stuff that happened in our life to do good stuff. The prodigal son of Luke chapter 15 certainly shows someone who walked away from all that was good, messed up his life, and then repented and came back. While there were repercussions for his failures, he was still reinstated as a son. In the book of Joel, a terrible swarm of locusts had devastated the land as a judgment brought on them for their sin. But God then promised that He would "give back the years that the locusts have eaten."

Let's summarize this a bit. So, how do we summarize? If both partners had a divorce for certain reasons, they are free to remarry. If not, things become less clear. We have always believed that God is the God of the future. While people certainly need to take responsibility for what they have done wrong and the consequences that a divorce brought against them, we have to believe that true repentance can right such a wrong before God. It is hard to believe that people are useless to God and unacceptable to Him because of this past failure. Further, it just does not seem consistent with what we read in the Bible about God. Each person must decide this for themselves based on what the Bible says.

Marriage forms the foundational element for a healthy society, the church believes low marriage standards are hurtful to individuals, to the family, and to the cause of Christ. Yet the prevalence of divorce in our culture demands that the church deal with this tragic issue. The strong feeling of the church against divorce grows out of the clear statement in the Bible that God hates divorce (Malachi 2:16) and that no human being should separate two persons joined together in holy matrimony. The reality of divorce forces the church to draw from Scripture guidelines for instances when God's ideal is not maintained.

The best guideline is whenever grace enables it is to forgive marital infidelity and seek healing in the marriage. This choice is especially desirable in cases where children would be further hurt and the family destroyed through divorce. Abandonment a long-term physical withdrawal from the home with neglect of the responsibilities, support, and duties required of one partner within a marriage would also prove the spouse's sinful conduct and could eventually allow for divorce.

Abuse poses another threat to marriages. Thousands of

women and in some cases men face serious beating and other forms of abuse from their spouses. God is concerned with the physical safety and well being of all. He does not look lightly upon such actions within marriage or families. In such circumstances a period of separation without divorce may be justified and useful for the healing of persons. If after serious attempts of counseling and reconciliation the abusing spouse departs rather than turning from actions of abuse.

1 Corinthians 7:12-15 But to the rest speak I, not the Lord: If any brother hath a wife that believeth not, and she be pleased to dwell with him, let him not put her away. And the woman which hath an husband that believeth not, and if he be pleased to dwell with her, let her not leave him. For the unbelieving husband is sanctified by the wife, and the unbelieving wife is sanctified by the husband: else were your children unclean; but now are they holy. But if the unbelieving depart, let him depart. A brother or a sister is not under bondage in such *cases:* but God hath called us to peace.

If there are biblical grounds that permit divorce, does that also justify remarriage? Though Old Testament Law permitted divorce, it placed limits on remarriage by prohibiting husbands from remarrying their former wives whom they had divorced. In a second marriage the wife was bound to the new marriage covenant. After forming the second marriage covenant she was not to go back to her first husband. The teaching of Jesus seems even more restrictive.

Sexual immorality is one of the biggest things that cause an end to marriage. Wherever possible, sexually immoral practices should be dealt with through repentance, confession, forgiveness, and reconciliation, thus saving the marriage. In no case does Jesus command divorce when unfaithfulness has occurred; He simply allows it. Nor did Jesus command remarriage when divorce has occurred. However, from Matthew 19:9 it seems that Jesus understood that the divorced will often remarry. Remarriage, like the first marriage, should be in the Lord This means with a Christian.

1 Corinthians 7:15 But if the unbelieving depart, let him depart. A brother or a sister is not under bondage in such *cases:* but God hath called us to peace.

When an unbelieving spouse is unwilling to remain in the marriage and initiates a divorce, the believer is set free from the marriage and can remarry if he or she so chooses without committing adultery. Where these exceptional circumstances exist, the question of remarriage must be resolved by the believer as he or she walks in the light of God's Word.

1 Corinthians 7:27, 28 Art thou bound unto a wife? seek not to be loosed. Art thou loosed from a wife? seek not a wife. But and if thou marry, thou hast not sinned; and if a virgin marry, she hath not sinned. Nevertheless such shall have trouble in the flesh: but I spare you.

Remarriage is a new contract or covenant. Even though the first covenant, because of sin, did not endure, the new covenant must be treated with all the love, commitment, and permanence the first marriage contract should have received.

At times, the primary victims of divorce and remarriage those abandoned and abused have been treated as outcasts in the church. However those who have gone through divorce, and in some cases remarriage, are persons God loves deeply. He does not show favoritism.

Romans 2:11 For there is no respect of persons with God.

James 2:1 My brethren, have not the faith of our Lord Jesus Christ, *the Lord* of glory, with respect of persons.

The church must receive with love and compassion all who are repentant and desire to follow Christ. Many today are living together rather than marrying because of the Churches stance on divorce. God constitutes living together as fornication. Couples living together, but unmarried should be instructed in the Bible's teaching on marriage and guided to observe God's law in forming a lifelong marriage covenant in Him.

Children are greatly victimized by the wake of divorce. I know this all to well. My Dad left my Mom when I was only one year of age. All too often a parent or parents who pursue divorce become so embroiled in meeting their own perceived personal needs, they never stop to consider the full impact of their actions on their children. To children, divorce brings great emotional trauma. The fallout is felt for years and in some cases a lifetime. Persons who find themselves contemplating divorce would do well to consider the full implications of such an action and its impact on children, extended family, and friends. The church is called to reach out to all who are hurt and love them as Jesus does...especially the children.

Matthew 18:1-6 At the same time came the disciples unto Jesus, saying, Who is the greatest in the kingdom of heaven? And Jesus called a little child unto him, and set him in the midst of them, And said, Verily I say unto you, Except ye be converted, and become as little children, ye shall not enter into the kingdom of heaven. Whosoever therefore shall humble himself as this little child, the same is greatest in the kingdom of heaven. And whoso shall receive one such little child in my name receiveth me. But whoso shall offend one of these little ones which believe in me, it were better for him that a millstone were hanged about his neck, and *that* he were drowned in the depth of the sea.

One concern has to do with the effect of divorce and remarriage upon the qualifications of those who would serve as pastors, ministers, elders, and deacons. Leaders are held to a high biblical standard. They are to conform to the requirement that they shall be the husband of one wife.

1 Timothy 3:2 A bishop then must be blameless, the husband of one wife, vigilant, sober, of good behaviour, given to hospitality, apt to teach;

1 Timothy 3:12 Let the deacons be the husbands of one wife, ruling their children and their own houses well.

Some have interpreted this phrase to mean the spiritual leader should not be a polygamist. But polygamy (marriage to multiple partners at the same time) was not practiced by first-century Jews or Christians, thereby eliminating this argument as a possible context for the apostle Paul's admonition. The Assemblies of God believes pastors and church leaders, should be those who have not been the guilty party in initiating a divorce. In situations where ministers are the unwilling recipients of divorce they are not to remarry because of their role as moral examples. Though the remarriage of divorced persons is called an act of adultery by Jesus, this does not mean that the remarried persons are living in a state of continuous adultery. Persons who have remarried and now understand

God's truth should be led to repentance for that sin and into a clear pattern of thinking about what the scripture teaches. They are not to divorce and return to their former marriages. Further divorce is a confusion of grace. Nothing is gained by committing another mistake in an attempt to rectify a previous sin. The Old Testament forbade a divorced and remarried partner from returning to the original partner. The divorced and remarried, no matter how grievous their past sin or faults, upon genuine repentance can be forgiven and restored to function in truth and integrity as part of God's family. Let the redeemed of the Lord say so.

Chapter Four
The Source of Divorce

The Source in this title is referring to the main reason why two people separate and divorce. We have all seen marriages crumble for a variety of reasons. Sometimes we are convinced that the wife has been a tramp or the husband a scumbag. Other situations seem to indicate that children or stepchildren have done all that they can to make life difficult and have maybe even worked to split up the parents. At other times, we attribute problems to everything from stressful job situations to meddling in-laws. For whatever reason, divorces occur. I want to give you a clear perspective on why divorces occur. We always want to find the fault of the other person when we all have to reflect on our part in this. Somebody did something; someone chose a behavior, and decisions were made that led to a divorce.

- infidelity
- impotence
- drug and alcohol abuse
- physical abuse
- personal growth

- finances
- parenting
- personal happiness
- intolerance and emotional abuse
- incompatibility

This is by no means everything but we will cover the majority of scenarios that people seem to face. Ask yourself where did you place fault and blame? If you are waiting for the correct answers, I hate to disappoint you, because the answers are not always as simple as checking a box. Sometimes, multiple boxes need to be checked, which I am sure that you discovered. Other times, you may have found yourself wanting to give an answer that wasn't among the choices that you were given. So, what is the cause of divorce? Well, as we have looked at a variety of situations, it would seem that the cause can be lots of different things like anger, infidelity, and so on. However, I want to submit to you that the cause is much more basic than the scenarios we have examined. You may have found yourself identifying different causes as to why marriages end. You may have come up with a list similar to the one above. And yet, none of those items listed are the cause of divorce but they are simply the manifestation of the cause. You see, in each and every situation the cause of divorce is selfishness! Yes, that's right. One cause with many manifestations. Take a minute and let that thought settle in. All that I am saying is that all divorce has its roots in selfishness. Selfishness is the cause of all divorces not necessarily your selfishness, but selfishness nonetheless.

Why do people have to polarize their view and see this as either, "I stay in the awful marriage and life continues to be horrendous and never gets any better," or "I get a divorce and all is well"? I've seen couples come in with this thinking, and I am always amazed that they never see a third possibility. If you have been divorced, try to set your own issues and situation aside as you review what happened. This is not the place for you to feel that you are being judged. Simply examine each situation objectively and see where selfishness is apparent. In Matthew 19, Jesus makes it clear that marriage was designed to be lifelong. He responds to the questions of the spiritual leaders by saying that divorce is due to hardness of our hearts. It is important to understand that our selfish desires, if pursued, can only be successful and rational if we adopt a hard-heart position. As you look at the situations, find the selfishness, find the hard heart, and you begin to understand the root of divorce.

Chapter Five Standing and Waiting

We must take from the Bible and utilize it's instructions. The Word of God is helpful with instruction regarding many aspects of marriage, particularly when it comes to separation, divorce, and restoration.

1 Corinthians 7:10, 11 And unto the married I command, *yet* not I, but the Lord, Let not the wife depart from *her* husband: But and if she depart, let her remain unmarried, or be reconciled to *her* husband: and let not the husband put away *his* wife.

This is about two powerful things standing and waiting. We are in such a hurry to move on and get our emotional needs met today. Standing and waiting does not work well at all with our seeming need for immediate pleasure, which we are all about. Paul says that we are not to find someone else tomorrow. Instead, we are to do the exact opposite. Tomorrow we are to wait, not find someone else, and work toward reconciliation with my spouse. As long as people wait and remain unmarried, reconciliation is still possible. I understand that you may be separated and experiencing the first no-conflict-days in years. It feels, and it seems good. However, God's desire for reconciliation with the power He will provide, is far better than just good; it is God's best. When we were first married, we had dreams and plans for a wonderful relationship and life together. Those first longings are still worth fighting for. My guess is that the deep longings you originally held are still buried somewhere deep down inside, and with some work are still accessible. So why do we have such difficulty with this wisdom? Get ready for the answer; you may not be happy with it. If I just throw away my old partner and meet someone new, I can have (in my own mind) a clean slate. In other words, I don't have to work on me or tackle my own issues. The new person doesn't know about all of the stuff buried in my closet, and for a while I can do a pretty good job of hiding them. If I stay in my current or old relationship, I will have to deal with my own stuff to bring about true reconciliation. I don't want to work that hard. And with this realization, they think that their marriage is healed. Hardly. But, again, it is a misunderstanding to think that reduced conflict is the same as an active, reconciled peace. Just as peace is active, so is waiting. Oftentimes, people get away from each other, have reduced conflict (which is nice), and then think that they will just wait until their feelings change before considering reconciliation. Many couples feel that a trial separation will help them get their feelings straightened out. They want to separate and have no contact to see if time apart will cause the warm feelings to return. Such a process is useless. Attitude and action must precede positive emotions. Distance alone will not turn emotions around.

Waiting is not something that we come by naturally in our culture. Whether we are in a line at the grocery store, caught in traffic, waiting our turn at Six Flags, we don't like to wait. We want to be waited upon quickly and efficiently. Yet, here I am asking you to wait. If you are a type A personality like me, waiting can seem not only difficult but also irrational.

We need to examine our behavior and make sure that it is honoring to both God and our spouse and not disciplinary in nature. I have seen Christians who have managed to justify cruel, toxic, spiteful behavior because of something that their spouse has done. Yet, there is never anything that our spouse can do that can make that behavior okay. You may believe that your spouse has done all kinds of awful things to hurt you. But as soon as you respond with hateful behavior, you may actually discover where the real problem lies. Who is the real you? Use this time to find out and to focus on loving behaviors even when it is hard. God is not in the business of asking you to do something that you cannot do. He knows that you are capable of loving the unloving, and this is your opportunity to do just that.

In the midst of a break-up what we need to be aware of is that you need others. When we are hurting, our natural tendency is to withdraw into our shell. This is counterproductive to what we need. We need others for support and care. We need safe people who we can lean on. I am speaking here of people of the same sex. The last thing that you need to do is to find support in someone of the opposite sex. It is too easy for that to go from crying on the shoulder to comfort in the arms of another. That is exactly what you don't need. But you do need reliable and faithful friends who you can count on; Friends who will listen, hold you accountable, comfort, and speak truth into your life.

Matthew 18:35 So likewise shall my heavenly Father do also unto you, if ye from your hearts forgive not every one his brother their trespasses.

I have seen many separated or divorced individuals who are completely unwilling to forgive their spouses for the wrongs that have been committed against them. How will God respond? This is a time of learning to understand the breadth of God's forgiveness in our lives and in turn learning to extend that to the person for whom we may feel such hatred. This step may take some time, so it is a good thing that we have some time while we are waiting.

Emotions seem to be out of control at any stage of separation or divorce. The feelings that we are experiencing toward our spouse, about ourselves, with regard to our hurt, and our fears about the future seem to take on a life of their own. It seems to be way more than I can even begin to deal with. So, I don't. I may shut down, become paralyzed, and crawl into a hole. Yet, this is not productive. Remember, we are determined to wait in an active, productive manner. So what can we do? Do not look at the rest of your life as one great unknown. Make plans for today. What can you do today that will be constructive? As you fill your days with meaningful activity, hope for the future will grow. As you come to understand yourself, develop yourself, accept yourself, you enhance the prospects of reconciliation with your spouse. Certainly every day will not always be emotionally easy and productive. But it is a game plan that will slowly prove to be more valuable than not, and with time and effort it will grow more consistent. Don't beat yourself up over the bad days. Cut yourself some slack. Suck it up during the bad days as a learning experience and become more healthy and productive tomorrow.

God has designed us for intimacy, especially intimacy with Him. As we become involved with our spouse, our kids, and our friends, God frequently gets relegated to some kind of Sunday ritual or morning routine. As we lose an important spousal relationship, we may find ourselves experiencing incredible loneliness. While I don't want to sound insensitive to your pain or overly spiritual, I want to make a point that loneliness is intensified because we have tried to use our spouse to meet needs that only God can. This may masquerade the void, but it never fills it. When our spouse is gone, our lack of intimacy with our creator is amplified. This waiting is the perfect opportunity for us to begin to truly get to know and connect with God in ways that we may never have before. Filling your need for intimacy with God frees you to cultivate relationships with your spouse and others from desire, as opposed to neediness, which is a much healthier place to be.

As you go through a time of separation or divorce, you may feel as though your life is founded on quick sand. There is no stability. If that is the case, then you know just how unstable and unpredictable that truly is. Becoming stable involves making good choices about behavior, enlisting the support of others, forgiving my spouse who has wronged me, tackling my out of control emotions and building an intimate, unshakeable relationship with God. It also requires being able to face yourself each day, acknowledging your situation, and stating, as I am going to make it work. I am going to balance my life out. You are not ready to be married until you are content to be single, that is, until you get both feet on the ground and establish yourself. We need a support system, and the best support system is Jesus Christ living in us through the Holy Spirit.

Philippians 4:13 I can do all things through Christ which strengtheneth me.

I am suggesting that you embrace life-changing, biblical truth.

Chapter Six
The Real Issues

Whether anyone in a relationship will admit it or not there are real issues we all will face. There are some realities that need to be acknowledged. I often overhear people refer to a situation and say, Well, it is what it is. Individuals going through an unwanted separation or divorce will often have great difficulty accepting what is taking place. They will fight it and deny its reality until the end of time. So, the first reality in facing issues is to accept your situation, whatever it may be, and determine a plan of action to move forward to the next step of your life. I am not talking about giving up and finding another relationship, but I am referring to the need to move forward in your own healing and growth.

Marriages fail most of the time because of a few main issues:

1st lack of an intimate relationship with God,

2nd lack of an intimate relationship with your mate, or

3rd lack of an intimate understanding and acceptance of yourself.

We sometimes believe that our only choice is to remain in a miserable marriage or else get a divorce. Yet, there is a third choice that often gets overlooked. You can fight for your marriage.

The reality is that failures in the past do not condemn your marriage for the future. Many couples say that there has just been too much pain, too much damage, and too much failure to ever be able to recover. Yet, this feeling and experience of failure can be turned into a marriage rebirth. Communication and levels of understanding can improve, and couples can actually find fulfillment in a relationship that once seemed destined for the trash heap. When couples have committed themselves to the process of reconciliation, I have seen many of them experience a marriage that is better than they have had in years and that they had been convinced was unachievable. Past failure does not prevent hope for the future.

You can only control and are only responsible for yourself. Your happiness is not dependent upon the actions and responses of your spouse. With hard work, many spouses will seemingly come to their senses. But not all do. You may walk through all of the steps that I have discussed. You may follow all of the reconciliation suggestions in the next chapter. You may honestly do all that you know to do, and do it all in a loving manner, only to find that your spouse has walked away. It could happen. But if it does, you will know that you have honestly tried everything possible. You will have honored God, your spouse, and will have grown healthier in the process. Just know that even when we do it all correctly, the results aren't always what we think they should be.

There is a time for holding on and there is a time for letting go. Knowing when your diligent efforts for reconciliation have not achieved their desired result is important. You may have done all that you could, and your spouse has still continued and successfully acquired his or her divorce. Now you must accept it. Of course, even then, this doesn't mean that reconciliation isn't still possible. I have seen couples re-dedicate or remarry after they have been apart for as long as five years. But for now, you must accept that you are divorced and move forward in being the person that God has called you to be. One final reality, and I want to stress that it is a reality.

Philippians 4:14 Notwithstanding ye have well done, that ye did communicate with my affliction.

Paul is not saying to be happy about your circumstances. That would be foolish and an absolute denial of reality. What he is saying is that, in spite of your circumstances, you can rejoice in the Lord. He is faithful, He will sustain, He will never leave us, He loves us, and He has forgiven us with a grace beyond what we can understand. He will redeem our life and, as hard as it may be to see in the moment, He will give us a future. Rejoice in the Lord always!

I believe in all that I have stated about the benefits of the standing and waiting process, I don't want to pretend that it is easy. I have been there. It is one of the most difficult and often painful things that you will ever do. There will be some days that you will declare it impossible, want to give up, and look for a quick emotional fix. There will be other days when it will seem more achievable. Your emotions will peak and valley and seem very undependable. During these times, cling to the Word and what you know as opposed to what you feel. Ask God to inhabit both your rational thoughts as well as your irrational feelings. Hang on to what you know to be true.

People will always say But you don't understand my situation!

God has not given us an alternative set of instructions that are different than those revealed to us through His Word. There is no alternate picture to view. But we go ahead and try to build our clever, theological scaffolding that is based upon our sin-based selfish desires. When we do so, we, and all those involved including God, are not truly satisfied. There may be a momentary feeling of reprieve, but this is far from fulfilled, God-pleasing satisfaction and holiness. The myths of our own ability to create something from disobedience that will honor God and people far exceed actuality. But the myth is a powerful attractor, and people frequently buy into the lie. People in pain make many statements that sound valid. And because people are in pain, we certainly want to be understanding and helpful. But we need to do so without compromising the truth of who God is.

I hear statements such as:

- "You deserve better."
- "I didn't seek God's will before I married the person."
- "I didn't know what I was getting into."
- "This isn't what I thought I was signing up for."
- "He/she is abusive physically, verbally, or psychologically."
- "I didn't listen to my parents or friends."
- "I need to be happy and fulfilled."
- "My spouse abuses alcohol or drugs."
- "My spouse uses pornography."
- "I've wasted enough years, and I am not staying any more."
- "I can't stand this anymore."
- "I can't do this anymore."
- "I shouldn't have to…"

All of these statements suggest feelings of understanding and sympathy. We don't want to be rigid, legalistic, and inflexible. We want to be people of grace. Yet, we have to be people of grace and love who are grounded in the truth. I have heard people proclaim that they were married to this or that person before they became a Christian. They didn't know any better, but now they do and therefore should be able to nullify the marriage and find someone else. In First Corinthians 7, Paul reaffirmed that God wants us to reconcile with our mates. We don't divorce them just because we became believers. Instead, we reconcile with them because we are now believers. When I hear comments like, "I can't stand this" or "I can't do this anymore," I can't help but wonder if their statements are true wouldn't that mean that God is a liar.

Philippians 4:13 I can do all things through Christ which strengtheneth me.

Paul assures us that there will not be more put on our plates than we can endure.

1 Corinthians 10:13 There hath no temptation taken you but such as is common to man: but God *is* faithful, who will not suffer you to be tempted above that ye are able; but will with the temptation also make a way to escape, that ye may be able to bear *it*.

God knows our limitations, and He will give us the strength, the wisdom, the stamina, and the endurance required to live in obedience to Him. He tells husbands to love their wives and wives to respect their husbands. Again, He doesn't tell us to do something that we can't. It is within our power to choose and to do, because He has given us the ability to do so.

CHAPTER SEVEN
A Transformed Mind

When you have a transformed mind you will better be positioned for God's best for you. You will not be consumed, defeated or allow the enemy to use your thoughts against you.

Romans 12:1, 2 I beseech you therefore, brethren, by the mercies of God, that ye present your bodies a living sacrifice, holy, acceptable unto God, *which is* your reasonable service. And be not conformed to this world: but be ye transformed by the renewing of your mind, that ye may prove what *is* that good, and acceptable, and perfect, will of God.

We have to be transformed by the Almighty, the Creator of the Universe. We must stop watching the world and adopting its methods of addressing difficult marriages. The world's view has led to pain, devastation, and the tearing apart of people's souls. Why would we choose to be conformed to that approach? But we continue to do so. This is why Paul says that we must be transformed by the renewing of our minds. When we do this, we will discover a very different perspective.

Many have expected a spouse to provide that which only God can give. Peace of mind, inner security, a confidence in the outcome of life, and a sense of joy about living do not come from marriage, but from an intimate relationship with God. God wants to be the absolute source of life for us. Truly, if He is our source, at the core, the very essence of who we are nothing can shake us. All of the seemingly commonsense comments fall right out the window. It's like this, "when I encounter seemingly insurmountable problems with my spouse, He is my source and strength for patience and love. When I hurt, He is my comfort. When I am exasperated, He is my peace. When I am unfairly accused, He is my truth. When I feel that I just can't do it anymore, He gives and is all I need to not just endure, but to be victorious over my situation. When I am transformed by the life-changing power of God."

I will be a part of the people that Paul describes in Colossians 3.

Colossians 3:1-3 If ye then be risen with Christ, seek those things which are above, where Christ sitteth on the right hand of God. Set your affection on things above, not on things on the earth. For ye are dead, and your life is hid with Christ in God.

Colossians 3:12-14 Put on therefore, as the elect of God, holy and beloved, bowels of mercies, kindness, humbleness of mind, meekness, longsuffering; Forbearing one another, and forgiving one another, if any man have a quarrel against any: even as Christ forgave you, so also *do* ye. And above all these things *put on* charity, which is the bond of perfectness.

God promises that He will do this if you will let Him. There is nothing more powerful than this truth. He can change your life and your marriage. God understands divorce, and He wants us to understand it and all of its devastating ramifications as well. He wants us to understand His heart in this matter. When we do, we will be prepared to love our mate as God intends and to build a marriage that reflects His love for us and absolutely glorifies Him in our lives!

Marriage was instituted by God.

Genesis 2:21-24 And the LORD God caused a deep sleep to fall upon Adam, and he slept: and he took one of his ribs, and closed up the flesh instead thereof; And the rib, which the LORD God had taken from man, made he a woman, and brought her unto the man. And Adam said, This *is* now bone of my bones, and flesh of my flesh: she shall be called Woman, because she was taken out of Man. Therefore shall a man leave his father and his mother, and shall cleave unto his wife: and they shall be one flesh.

He created a wife for Adam and ordained marriage because He deemed that it was not good for man to be alone. God created a suitable helper to assist Adam in ruling the earth, raising a family, and worshiping God.

Marriage is to be a single relationship between one man and one woman. God gave Adam just one wife. Polygamy was practiced during the Old Testament era, but this never made for happy homes and was not in keeping with God's original design.

Marriage is to be a heterosexual relationship. God created Eve (a female) for Adam (a male).

Genesis 1:27 So God created man in his *own* image, in the image of God created he him; male and female created he them.

Genesis 2:22 And the rib, which the LORD God had taken from man, made he a woman, and brought her unto the man.

There is nothing in Genesis about Adam and Steve!

Genesis 1:28 And God blessed them, and God said unto them, Be fruitful, and multiply, and replenish the earth, and subdue it: and have dominion over the fish of the sea, and over the fowl of the air, and over every living thing that moveth upon the earth.

Marriage involves formally and publicly leaving one's own parents in order to establish a new family as a married couple. The ceremonies, and formalities vary from culture to culture, but there must be a public recognition of the couple's intent to marry. This seems to be inherent in the concept of leaving.

Marriage is a relationship that binds a couple until death. This is implicit in the concept of cleaving being glued together or bound in a one-flesh relationship. Jesus and Paul explicitly taught that the marriage relationship can only be broken by death.

Mark 10:9 What therefore God hath joined together, let not man put asunder.

1 Corinthians 7:39 The wife is bound by the law as long as her husband liveth; but if her husband be dead, she is at liberty to be married to whom she will; only in the Lord.

Romans 7:2, 3 For the woman which hath an husband is bound by the law to *her* husband so long as he liveth; but if the husband be dead, she is loosed from the law of *her* husband. So then if, while *her* husband liveth, she be married to another man, she shall be called an adulteress: but if her husband be dead, she is free from that law; so that she is no adulteress, though she be married to another man.

Marriage involves the headship of the husband over the wife. This is suggested by Adam's priority in the order of creation and in the naming of Eve. The apostle Paul clearly spells out the headship of the husband.

Ephesians 5:23 For the husband is the head of the wife, even as Christ is the head of the church: and he is the saviour of the body.

1 Corinthians 11:3 But I would have you know, that the head of every man is Christ; and the head of the woman *is* the man; and the head of Christ *is* God.

God created Adam and placed him in The Garden of Eden with the assigned task of taking care of it. God very quickly recognized that it was not good for man to be alone.

Genesis 2:18 And the LORD God said, *It is* not good that the man should be alone; I will make him an help meet for him.

A child partakes of the flesh of both the father and the mother, and the two are absolutely undividable!

Matthew 19:6 Wherefore they are no more twain, but one flesh. What therefore God hath joined together, let not man put asunder.

There is no doubt in my mind that He added this statement because humanity had been making such a mess of the design, trying to find things to fit their own selfish desires. Jesus made it clear that God alone has the right and power to appoint the beginning and end of marriage. Until a marriage is broken by the death of one of the partners, the couple should heed the words of Jesus. But other than the additional statement, note that the plan had not changed since the creation of the world. It was still about a man and a woman leaving their parents and uniting, becoming one flesh, for a lifetime of companionship. Regardless of this, we find ourselves in a new day where divorce is an everyday reality. While divorce was uncommon today, it is an accepted, almost expected, form of family structure. We best address it head on. We might as well acknowledge it and see what God says about it.

This is where the subject of marriage and divorce gets a little tricky as we examine God's Word. What happens when we decide that we have had enough of the other person, and we no longer want to be married? What happens when we find ourselves divorced and want to consider remarriage? When we have children from a previous marriage, and we choose to remarry, how do we prioritize the relationships? These are very important questions to which we must have answers. Surely we can go to the Scriptures and find crystal clear guidelines or so we hope. Yet, when we go to the Scriptures to research this subject and look for the blueprint, we are typically disappointed that there is almost no information. This lack of material has created numerous books as authors try to glean a few truths from subtle implications in Scripture. Many have tried to take general principles and interpret. As we might imagine, the result is a host of opinions that range from one extreme to the other with little concrete, scriptural support. The frustrating reality is this: God's Word spells out a very clear plan for the perfect marriage. That is His plan. There is no other plan because He has clearly told us what He desires us to do is His plan. Anything else is against His design. Some individuals have adopted a position that if they divorce their spouse, and just remain unmarried, then all is good. They figured that the marriage was not good, and that an unhappy, incompatible marriage was probably a greater sin than divorce. Scripture does not support this conclusion. Instead, it teaches a core principle that marriage is right, and the disruption of marriage is wrong. Without getting into a discussion of remarriage at this point, I do want to emphasize what God emphasizes. The bond that Scripture talks about between a husband and wife is significant. When Jesus says that the two will be come one flesh, He is using the Greek word that literally means that the two people are glued together. In marriage identities have become intertwined. They are bonded glued together. The ripping and tearing that occurs in the closure of this marriage is massively painful. People exhibit many of the symptoms of a human organism under deep stress. Is there any evidence or information that might constitute pieces of another plan? Yes, there is some, but even this is geared to maintain the original marriage not to pursue something else.

In others words, even if the marriage is disrupted, Paul said that the goal is to restore it back to a glued and bonded state. Any elements of an alternate plan are never for the purpose of ending a marriage and moving on to the next. I want to mention here that second marriages and third and fourth marriages don't seem to fix the problems encountered in the first. One of the leading causes of failure in remarriage is the effect on the children. Children always remain loyal to their birth parents. They will can cause trouble for stepparents. It is difficult for the children to get their parents back together. But they try… I've heard too many divorced parents say, I wish I knew then what I know now. Gradually, I have come to the conclusion that divorce is not the answer. It doesn't necessarily solve the problems it attempts to solve. Most marriages are worth saving….I've grown increasingly convinced that most marriages are worth saving simply because most problems are solvable. Adults, in their pursuit of pain-free, comfortable happiness, may not always realize that most children see divorce as the most pivotal, central event of their lives. Marriage is a relationship that we commit ourselves to with lifelong stability. Yet, as problems arise and they will, the seeming durability quickly changes into conditional commitment complete with a bailout clause. Can you imagine how this would look if we applied this exit strategy to other permanent relationships specifically our children? Divorcing our children is not an option even when they prevent our goals and plans, even when they behave in ways we never would have dreamed of. Imagine an overwhelmed parent announcing, I'm divorcing my son on the grounds of extreme mental cruelty. Instead, we learn to readjust, to modify our expectations, and roll with the punches. We become grateful for the good times and learn to expect the hard times. Marriage vows are also taken without marriage manuals. Entering marriage with unrealistic expectations can eventually kill the relationship, and it often does. Unlike the committed, all-forgiving attitude we have toward our children, when our mates fail to live up to our expectations, we consider divorce as an option. While the example of divorcing our children may sound absurd, in light of God's design for marriage, divorcing our mates should seem just as absurd to us. We appear determined to have another plan and equally determined to make it work. When it doesn't work, we sometimes continue to push through and pretend that it is working even when we know better. It is easy to forget that What you are, as a parent, will to a large extent be what your children will become....How you handle your relationships with your spouse and your children will teach them how to handle major difficulties in their own lives. If you find yourself having difficulty with God's plan, I want to strongly encourage you to search God's Word for His answers and to seek Godly counsel. I have seen too many individuals, who are in a trying marriage, simply get out because it is what their feelings dictate that they do. Seeking the Lord, studying, trusting, and submitting are all too difficult. We can't shift the responsibility to someone else. If we obtained poor counsel, we are responsible. We are not excused. Eve tried this approach in The Garden by blaming her sin on the serpent, and it didn't work. As Christians, we like to talk about our loving God, who is full of grace for His flawed, and often failing, children.

I sometimes hear Christians talk about not judging each other. Someone will say It is wrong to lie, steal, commit adultery, practice homosexuality, and so on, only to have someone else say, It is not our place to judge; it is God's. That is true. But when they make a statement such as that presented, is it a judgment? God is the one who has proclaimed absolutes of right and wrong. It is absurd to think that quoting God's Word is judgmental! The Word is filled with God's pure and simple judgments. Our God is indeed a God of love and grace. He is also a God who draws boundaries of right and wrong, can be displeased, and hates certain things. Here are a few,

- God hates haughty eyes. (See Proverbs 6:17.)
- God hates a lying tongue. (See Proverbs 6:17.)
- God hates hands that shed innocent blood. (See Proverbs 6:17.)
- God hates a heart that devises wicked schemes. (See Proverbs 6:18.)
- God hates feet that run rapidly to evil. (See Proverbs 6:18.)
- God hates false witnesses who utter lies. (See Proverbs 6:19.)
- God hates one who stirs up dissension among brothers. (See Proverbs 6:19.)
- God hates it when sacrifices are burned to other gods. (See Jeremiah 44:4-5.)
- God hates a man's covering himself with violence. (See Malachi 2:16.)
- God's hates divorce. (See Malachi 2:16.) This last passage in Malachi is significant and enlightening regarding the importance that God places on marriages and relationships. Let's look at this amazingly clear and powerful section of Scripture.

Malachi 2:10 Have we not all one father? hath not one God created us? why do we deal treacherously every man against his brother, by profaning the covenant of our fathers?

Malachi 2:13-16 And this have ye done again, covering the altar of the LORD with tears, with weeping, and with crying out, insomuch that he regardeth not the offering any more, or receiveth *it* with good will at your hand. Yet ye say, Wherefore? Because the LORD hath been witness between thee and the wife of thy youth, against whom thou hast dealt treacherously: yet *is* she thy companion, and the wife of thy covenant. And did not he make one? Yet had he the residue of the spirit. And wherefore one? That he might seek a godly seed. Therefore take heed to your spirit, and let none deal treacherously against the wife of his youth. For the LORD, the God of Israel, saith that he hateth putting away: for *one* covereth violence with his garment, saith the LORD of hosts: therefore take heed to your spirit, that ye deal not treacherously.

It is obvious that God considers it a major disaster when we break faith with our spouse. He considers this a sacred bond that is not to be broken. When it is, it doesn't just affect our relationship with our spouse, but God indicates that it impacts our very relationship with Him. We break faith with our spouse, then, in our pain, loneliness, and confusion, we come before God with tears. We cry out when He doesn't seem to pay attention to us. We seem confused and don't understand why He seems so far away. I think that God must shake His head at our seeming inability to understand why our relationship with Him has changed. He determines the beginning by the commencement of the marriage. He stands as the witness to our proclamation of lifelong faith to the other. He is at the heart of the glue that binds us together. And He is saying, ever so clearly, I have witnessed this covenant. The manner in which you treat and love your spouse is so important that it will impact your very relationship with Me.

Whoever commits himself or herself to God must also honor his or her lifelong commitment to his or her spouse. God expects us to love our brother in order to be able to truly love Him. He also expects us to maintain our commitment and faith to our spouse if we are to be able to keep such with Him as well. I believe that is clear. No matter what I have to teach God's best plan above all else. This book is not to give you the bullet to destroy your marriage for selfish reasons. I think this is consistent with the spirit of God's Word. God doesn't just hate divorce because of what it says about our ability to keep our word and our commitment. God hates divorce because of what it does to people he loves! He hates the deception, the breach of faith, the long-lasting agony that is part and parcel of divorce. He hates what it does to the children too....If you're a parent, imagine watching your child go through an experience that would tear at the child's soul and cause deep and lasting pain. Wouldn't you hate anything that would hurt your child this badly? Most parents would.

Jesus responded that we do have a choice. We may indeed decide that if there is no other plan, we don't want to run the risk of a divorce and the impact that could have on our relationships with God and others. But if we decide to marry, then we do so understanding that next to our commitment to God, our marriage commitment is the most important and significant relationship in which we will enter. It will require consistent work and an understanding and acceptance of certain principles. Building a strong spiritually based marriage requires a willingness to bring every thought into captivity and conform every behavior to the standard of God's truth. Remember God understands us, and He does not give us, or ask of us, more than we can handle. He only gives us a single plan for marriage, because He knows that with His help, it is a doable plan. Engaging in and maintaining a plan A marriage requires a no-turning-back mindset. The covenantal seal is meant to designate the irrevocable nature of the relationship.

An irrevocable commitment to covenant-keeping and a moment by- moment guarding of the seal are absolute prerequisites for those who wish to place and keep their marriages on a solid spiritual foundation. This is God's Plan! If you haven't set the escape way on fire, it is time to do so!

Chapter Eight
Reflection is Important

Reflection of how we see ourselves and how God sees us is very important. Let us take it a step farther how do you view God? I know that may seem like a strange question, but it is an important one. Some view God as an all powerful being that is constantly waiting for us to mess up. As a result, they see themselves as wavering between being saved one minute and lost the next. God seems to be looking for a way to kick them out of heaven.

God's agenda is not to condemn and kick people out. If that were the case, then He didn't need to send His son. Based upon the law that God had given humankind, and humanity's blatant disregard for it, He was more than justified to kick us all out. But again, that is not His agenda. He has chosen to reach out to us with Jesus to bridge the sin gap so that we might enter a secure relationship with Him for all of eternity.

John 1:12, 13 But as many as received him, to them gave he power to become the sons of God, *even* to them that believe on his name: Which were born, not of blood, nor of the will of the flesh, nor of the will of man, but of God.

By God's choice, we have been made His children, and being a child is a secure relationship. We are His children and are even more secure with Him than our own children are with us.

2 Corinthians 1:21, 22 Now he which stablisheth us with you in Christ, and hath anointed us, *is* God; Who hath also sealed us, and given the earnest of the Spirit in our hearts.

We are owned by God, and we bear His seal of ownership, and that seal marks His guarantee of what is to come. Notice Paul doesn't say, You are in Christ for awhile, and God really hopes that good things will come your way. No, he says we are sealed, and His Spirit is our guarantee of the future. You can't get much more solid than that. As God's child, I am more than aware of what a flawed and disgraceful mess I can be. I can't even imagine how the God of the universe could even listen to my prayers, let alone call me friend. For this reason, I find the encouraging words in Philippians meet me right where I live. Paul writes that he is confident of this,

Philippians 1:6 Being confident of this very thing, that he which hath begun a good work in you will perform *it* until the day of Jesus Christ:

He didn't write that God would discard me unless I get it together and straighten up. No, Paul says that God began a good work in me and refused to stop with just beginning the work. He will not abandon me!

We have talked about the power of reflection as well as the grace of God. I certainly hope that you are moved by the discussion of God's grace and His offer to you. But you are probably still wondering how these discussions made their way into a book about marriage and divorce. Hang with me, and I promise in this next section to put the pieces together.

Ephesians 5:22-24 Wives, submit yourselves unto your own husbands, as unto the Lord. For the husband is the head of the wife, even as Christ is the head of the church: and he is the saviour of the body. Therefore as the church is subject unto Christ, so *let* the wives *be* to their own husbands in every thing.

I often find that the men are happy about this verse. The passage has been abused in ways that were never intended. He wrote nearly 2000 years ago, simply expressing truths about God's design for the family. He said that in God's design, there are structural roles that function best. And in that context, he says that wives are to submit to their husbands as though they are submitting to the Lord. Similarly the husband's relationship to the wife as Christ is to the Church. This is not a mere outward expression, but is an inward attitude. The problem is that men have used this passage to demand that a wife bow to his every word and obey whatever he says. No wonder women get upset with Paul over this passage. However, it needs to be clearly understood that this kind of relationship is not what Paul is talking about. He does acknowledge that in God's design the husband is head of the house and the wife is to acknowledge that role. The problem is that simply bossing others around doesn't make a man the head of anything. He merely demonstrates his expertise at being a jerk. Demanding that everyone shrink to his authority does not mean that he is leading as Christ leads the Church. Many men love to read this passage and stop. That is the problem. When you look at what comes next, you begin to realize why men don't want to read any farther and why the wife was actually given the easier role. You begin to understand the kind of leadership that Paul wants a wife to submit to.

Ephesians 5:25-31 Husbands, love your wives, even as Christ also loved the church, and gave himself for it; That he might sanctify and cleanse it with the washing of water by the word, That he might present it to himself a glorious church, not having spot, or wrinkle, or any such thing; but that it should be holy and without blemish. So ought men to love their wives as their own bodies. He that loveth his wife loveth himself. For no man ever yet hated his own flesh; but nourisheth and cherisheth it, even as the Lord the church: For we are members of his body, of his flesh, and of his bones. For this cause shall a man leave his father and mother, and shall be joined unto his wife, and they two shall be one flesh.

This is powerful. A man is not to play boss, making demands, and insisting that everything is his way. He is to love his wife as Christ loves the church and gave His life for her. Paul states that as a husband, men are to lay down their lives for their wives.

While that is important and honorable, Paul is talking way beyond that. He is saying that men should even give up their lives, give up their desires, and give up the things that they want for the purpose of loving a woman.

Physically dying is one thing, but a man giving up his life for his wife is entirely different and can be much harder. Now how can we do that? Certainly it won't happen by being the boss who demands his own way. It is going to happen when we learn to love our wives as our own bodies. Men, you have been given a difficult charge that will require all of who you are. That is what being a husband is all about. If men and women would truly grasp the equal but different roles that God has given them, they would find it easier to fulfill them if their mate were also coming to the table honoring God's design. While I want you to grasp the significance of this passage in terms of our roles with each other, there is a larger point that I want to make.

Ephesians 5:32, 33 This is a great mystery: but I speak concerning Christ and the church. Nevertheless let every one of you in particular so love his wife even as himself; and the wife *see* that she reverence *her* husband.

I want you to notice that Paul has taught that men are to love their wives, and women are to respect their husbands. This is a reminder that we are not talking about some subjective feelings that come and go. We don't always have control over what we feel. But we do have control over what we do. Paul wouldn't ask us to do something that we have no control over. He has stated that we are to love and we are to respect, and because these are choices of behavior, we absolutely are capable to doing them. He is presenting a clear picture that our marriages are a reflection. Christ loves the Church and gave His all for her. Husbands are to reflect that sacrificial relationship. The Church is to submit to and respect Christ's headship, just as the wife is to do with regard to her husband. In other words, people should be able to look at our marriages and see a reflection. They should be able to stand back, observe us, and gain an understanding of God's relationship to His people. Our marriages are a testimony of how God relates to His people, or at least they were meant to be. But how are we doing? Do our marriages bear witness to that fact? Unfortunately, with a divorce rate in the Church that equals or exceeds that of the world, it is clear that we are getting in the way and pursuing our own agendas rather than being a reflection of what God desires. Rather than look at our marriages and see an example of God's continuous love for His people, nonbelievers are more likely to walk away with a belief that God just throws His people away when He tires of them and finds other people. When they become difficult to deal with, He gets rid of them. When they no longer please Him, they are gone.

As the Body of Christ, we bear the image of God on the earth to others around us. Unbelievers look at the Body of Christ to see who God is and what He is like. When we, as the body of Christ, embrace the values of society around us rather than Jesus' values, we slander the character of Christ in the sight of those around us and become a stumbling block and hindrance to their salvation. Unfortunately, the breakup of a marriage is a reflection on God also a false reflection. The divorce of two married people makes the false claim that God is not one after all, because people are made in His image. Will Christ ever break the relationship between himself and His church? Absolutely not! Will Christ ever be divorced or separated from the believer? NO!

Since the marriage union is a picture of the permanent relationship between Christ and His church, the marriage union itself must be permanent. Today's wedding ceremonies often include vows that the couple has created. Yet, even then many of the traditional phrases are still retained because of the significance they have communicated throughout generations. The most often repeated vows include some form of the following: Do you promise to **love**, **honor**, and **cherish** this person **in sickness** and **in health**, for **richer** for **poorer**, for **better** and for **worse**, as **long as you both shall live**? It is a short question that is packed with commitments that carry huge ramifications. Let's examine some of the key words. We begin by promising. The question then becomes is your word good? If it isn't, several things can happen. Our marriage vows are possibly the most important human promise that we will ever make. Will you keep your promise? You have promised to love, honor, and cherish your spouse. Again, these are not sentimental, gooey feelings. They are decisions about how you will choose and commit to behave. As you stand before the altar, the minister, or the justice of the peace, you look at your beautiful or handsome spouse, and you easily say the words of a promise that, at the moment, seem easy to keep. Yet, most vows wisely include conditions that will challenge the best of promises. You will notice that we commit to loving in sickness and in health. Here I am at the altar, you say. He seems pretty healthy to me. Sickness isn't an issue. This will be an easy statement to follow through on. What about when an unexpected disease is discovered? When aging deteriorates his body, how will you react? We promise to love and cherish for richer or poorer. Obviously we have enough money to get married. We have jobs and can afford nice things. Poorer shouldn't be a problem so I can sign up for that. Yet, how will you respond if your spouse is laid off from work due to a recession in the economy or as a result of outsourcing? What if he or she cannot find another job? When we are employed, in good health, and life seems good, we can easily pronounce these words of lifelong commitment. It is not difficult. But the very reason that we say, in sickness and in health, for richer or poorer, for better or worse is because, rest assured, there can be sickness, poorer, and worse. To ignore this reality is not a good idea. It is when we are in the middle of those times that we find out what our promise of love, cherish, and honor are made of. During these difficult, challenging, and sometimes horrendous times, a person's depth of character is revealed. When things are going the way that we believe that they ought, life is good and smiling is easy.

I suppose the same question could be asked of God. He has promised to love us as His children and He has promised that nothing can separate us from that. But what about when we are rebellious, disobedient, mean-spirited, arrogant, proud and deeply hurting the other children that God loves? Does He say, Well, yes, I promised to love you, but that was before you became all of these things that are unlovable. Now I have changed My mind and it is a different story? Thank God that He doesn't do that. One great unchanging truth is this things change. How will I deal with them when they do? I have seen marriages end because a wife put on 40 extra pounds, because he or she had an affair, a husband didn't make enough money to satisfy his wife's taste, a wife unexpectedly came down with a devastating, terminal illness, a husband lost his job, or because a child was born with special needs. All of these situations and more fit under the umbrella of in sickness and in health, for richer or poorer, for better for worse. I have also been privileged to see marriages survive the same list of problems. Committed spouses deal with and weather difficult changes. Frequently they do more than that. Many have grown stronger, healed, and soared as they allowed God to redeem and restore what had become ugly and repulsive. God is not in the business of discarding and throwing us away. Rather, He specializes in healing, making new, and restoring.

2 Corinthians 5:18 And all things *are* of God, who hath reconciled us to himself by Jesus Christ, and hath given to us the ministry of reconciliation;

Understanding that we are a reflection is critical to our understanding of marriage and its purposes. We are called to accurately reflect God to the world around us. God's relationship with us is based upon a permanent, relentless, never-ending love. He fully knows us and then, by choice, unconditionally loves us fully. He has placed love in our lives to reflect to those around us. We are truly a reflection to other couples, to each other, to our children, to other Christians, as well as to nonbelievers. This reflection, whether we want it to or not, tells a story: a story of God's love and relationship with His people. If your marriage tells of a God who is conditional, then you are telling your story. However, if your marriage paints a picture of a God who never leaves, then you are reflecting God and His story.

CHAPTER NINE
God's Bride

For us to understand all this even better is to comprehend us as God's Bride even before our marriage to a man or woman. From the very beginning, God designed people for intimacy with Himself. Adam walked through The Garden in the cool of the evening with God. What an image the created walks and talks with the Creator. It would be wonderful to have even been just an ear in those conversations what did they talk about? Were they discussing plans for the future of the world? What kinds of questions did Adam have for God? What an opportunity to be with the Creator! You most likely know what happened in The Garden and the resulting breach in the relationship. This placed humanity in a broken and distant position with God. Yet, God had certainly not given up on people; He had a plan. We see in Scripture in which God's plan unfolded as He chose His bride by selecting an individual, Abraham, who would become a people of a nation. God made covenants with humanity an agreement, a contract. One of those early agreements was made with Noah. The earth had become a very godless and corrupt place. It didn't seem that there was much worth salvaging. Yet, God found one righteous man and gave him very clear instructions concerning what he needed to do to survive the coming catastrophe. Following the flood, God made a covenant with Noah regarding this issue of flooding He would never again destroy the entire world with a flood. We see God called Abraham. God could have selected anybody that He wanted. God made a covenant with Abraham.

Genesis 15:5 And he brought him forth abroad, and said, Look now toward heaven, and tell the stars, if thou be able to number them: and he said unto him, So shall thy seed be.

God selected an individual who would become a nation who would become God's bride. This covenant was confirmed again. The covenant was carried on with Jacob, who literally became Israel, and Israel became the bride of God. What an awesome privilege and opportunity, to be selected as the favored people of the Creator. It wasn't long before Israel became complacent and self-centered and took the Creator of the Universe for granted. God used Moses to lead the Israelites out of their captivity. Yet, by the time they got to the Red Sea, they were already complaining. They grumbled about food; then water; and by the end they were ready to forsake God for another. Israel had been unfaithful to her husband. Yet, even after severe consequences when you think that she would have seen the error of her ways, when you think she would have learned her lesson this was only the beginning of her problems. God loved Israel as His wife. Even when she sinned, if she repented and returned, God took her back time and time again. Yet she never seemed to quite grasp the concept of faithfulness and trust in her Husband.

What an amazing pattern Israel continued to sin against and stray from her husband; God punished and yet pleaded for the nation to return; Israel repented and returned; God blessed Israel; and then they walked away again, thus repeating the pattern. It made no sense. They found no fault in God, but they forsook Him.

Jeremiah 2:35 Yet thou sayest, Because I am innocent, surely his anger shall turn from me. Behold, I will plead with thee, because thou sayest, I have not sinned.

This pattern has implications for our own marriages and will be addressed later in the book. But for right now, it is important to see that after a continued unrepentant lifestyle of unfaithfulness, God gave Israel her certificate of divorce. This was no arbitrary in the heat of the moment impulse. God had dealt with Israel's pattern of unfaithfulness for years and years. He realized that she was not going to change. So, He filed for divorce. Yet, even in the midst of this, He continued to plead and offer restoration.

Jeremiah 3:11-14 And the LORD said unto me, The backsliding Israel hath justified herself more than treacherous Judah. Go and proclaim these words toward the north, and say, Return, thou backsliding Israel, saith the LORD; *and* I will not cause mine anger to fall upon you: for I *am* merciful, saith the LORD, *and* I will not keep *anger* for ever. Only acknowledge thine iniquity, that thou hast transgressed against the LORD thy God, and hast scattered thy ways to the strangers under every green tree, and ye have not obeyed my voice, saith the LORD. Turn, O backsliding children, saith the LORD; for I am married unto you: and I will take you one of a city, and two of a family, and I will bring you to Zion:

Many people have experienced the pain of an unfaithful spouse. Yet, I wonder how many have experienced repeated unfaithfulness over the span of many years as God did. Some, I am certain, but not most. It becomes quite clear that God was grieved at the loss of His beloved. Not only does He understand divorce, but He also understands all of the accompanying pain. He understands the complications, the anger, the issues, the embarrassment, the betrayal and rejection, the longings, and all of the other associated hurts. He understands it, because He has experienced it. God knows the impact that divorce has on people because it has impacted Him. God even knows what it is like, and how difficult it is to initiate divorce, because He had to initiate it. God understands divorce. I know this may be a difficult concept to get your head around. We usually don't think of God having to deal with this kind of an issue. We think that He is busy keeping the stars in place and making sure the earth tilts the right direction. But feeling hurt and pain, understanding where I live day in and day out we tend to think that God is out of touch with these kinds of issues. Know that He is not. So, what is your situation? Has your spouse been unfaithful? God knows that pain better than anyone. Has your spouse said one thing and done another? Israel fits there. Have you pleaded and tried everything that you know how to do in order to save your marriage? So did God. Were you the one who had to begin the divorce proceedings because you had run out of options? God knows how difficult that is. Or perhaps your spouse has decided to leave the marriage for no apparent reason. You have been a faithful husband or wife. You have done your best to meet your spouse's needs, offering love and kindness at each turn. Your spouse truly has nothing against you. As a matter of fact, your spouse has had to work to manufacture some twisted justification for these actions. How awful is that? God has been in the same place. But wait a minute what about property issues? God never had to deal with dividing who gets what and the unfairness that can accompany this. The very city that God gave to Israel with instructions for His temple, He had to watch be destroyed. This was significant. And what about child custody? The prophets, God's messengers, went to Israel pleading God's case. These sinful, guilty people lied to the prophets, as we saw in Jeremiah, claiming that they had done nothing wrong. As Jerusalem was destroyed, as the people lived in exile, as segments of the population were taken into captivity, as all of this happened God had to watch. Israel took her unfaithfulness to a new level, and therefore could no longer be married to God. Yet in this process, God watched innocent children live in brokenness, pain, hunger, and misery, while they were homeless and lost. This grieved God's heart. This was not what He wanted. These were not the plans that He had for His bride. He had told Israel repeatedly the limitless blessings that He would bestow upon her if she simply remained faithful. He desired to be a loving husband to her. All she had to do was let Him. But regardless of the breadth and depth of His love, she still chose a different course. It made absolutely no sense. Logical or not, it was still the choice that she made. You may have thought up to now that no one understands you, that no one gets what you have gone or are going through. Believe me God gets it. He understands all of your pain in your situation. He understands what divorce does to people and more specifically, He understands what it has done to you.

Chapter Ten Creative Reasoning

When we fall in deception that is brought by the enemy we must use creative reasoning. Satan is the master of deception, the ultimate author of excuses, and can weave a rationalization. He is amazingly helpful in assisting us in doing the same, and oh how good we have gotten at it. Satan knows the truth, and he knows how to lie. He is the chief crafter of taking an part of truth and shaping it into something that looks reasonable, that makes logical sense, and then stuffing it with absolute heresy.

Many of us think that God wants us to be happy so yes, you are miserable in your marriage, and yes, God really doesn't want you to live that way. I will get a divorce because God wants me to be happy. This thinking originates from the father of lies himself satan. Satan began this lie quite early, Adam and Eve had a pretty good set-up in The Garden, hanging out with God and enjoying the beauty and fruit of The Garden. The Garden of Eden was the timeshare resort to end all resorts. God gave them a relatively simple and clear instruction you can eat of any tree in The Garden, except the Tree of Knowledge of Good and Evil. Why couldn't they stay within these boundaries? God gave Adam and Eve every tree and fruit they could possibly want with but one restriction. God said that the consequence would be death if they ate from that tree. So, what happened? Satan came along and had a conversation with them. He asked them how things were going, what they had been up to, and how the sampling of the fruit was going? They related to him that they could eat of any tree in the garden except the Tree of Knowledge of Good and Evil. Satan asked them what was up with that. They related the consequences that God warned them about. Satan responded, scoffing in disbelief that they would be so stupid as to buy such a line. He appealed to their sense of getting what they wanted and being happy. Now here comes the construction of the poison. You've got to be kidding me! Did He really tell you that you would die? That's not going to happen. Take a bite and see. Besides He is just trying to keep you from being happy. Listen, if you will eat from that fruit bar, you will become smarter than you ever imagined and life will really be great for you. Is there a component of truth in this rationalization? Of course! As we know from a hindsight perspective, satan was correct in that they didn't actually die as soon as they ate of the tree. We also know that their eyes were opened and there was an increase in knowledge and awareness. The outside chocolate looks pretty good. But what was the filling on the inside? After eating the forbidden fruit, they began the aging and dying process that would eventually culminate in their actual death. Yes, they gained knowledge, and with it came a loss of innocence that they could never regain. They were kicked out of The Garden, and life became a pretty intense journey with lots of hard work and pain from then on. They thought that they would be happier if they did what seemed best to them, even though it was in direct disobedience to God. However, they quickly realized that obedience to God's instructions would have left them in a far better place than they found themselves after the Original Sin. In other words, had they obeyed, they would have been happier. Scripture is very clear that God's priority for us is holiness, not happiness. For some reason, this seems to be a difficult concept for us to grasp. And yet, if we could learn to wrap our brains around this, we would find that by choosing holiness, happiness has a much better chance of following. I am not saying that you will always be happy if you do the right thing. That is oftentimes not true. But I will say that if you choose what appears to be happiness over holiness, you will ultimately be very dissatisfied. Happiness is such a short-lived feeling. Yes it is nice to feel happy, and it is great to enjoy those moments. But it is amazing how much effort and focus we place on something that is so brief, and how little attention we give to the things that have long-term consequences. When are you most pleased when your child gets drunk and enjoys a few moments of outward abandon and happiness with his or her friends, or when your child makes the right and responsible choice that you know will benefit him or her long-term? Our Father is no different. He loves us and wants our absolute best. When we take away the excuse, we will discover the truth.

I am very, very aware of the complications of marriage, how badly things can hurt, and how alone you can feel. I know that marriages can be more than challenging. So I assure you that I am not offering some commonplace such as, Just stay and be good and all will turn out happily ever after. If only it were that simple. But I am telling you the truth when I say that God desires your obedience over your focused pursuit of happiness.

I believe that God's Word confirms that the only actual chance that I have for long-term satisfaction (far superior to short-lived moments of happiness) will come as a result of my intentional decision to obey Him in the most difficult of situations. Obedience is work. Obedience involves trusting God's love enough to obey Him even when I don't understand. I can tell you that I have never regretted making the decision to obey. However, when I have disobeyed because my logic seemed to have a better idea of how to achieve happiness, it has come back to bite me without fail. God desires a relationship with us based upon love and trust. He doesn't need us to do great deeds of service nearly as much as He needs us to live an authentically obedient relationship.

1 Samuel 15:22 And Samuel said, Hath the LORD *as great* delight in burnt offerings and sacrifices, as in obeying the voice of the LORD? Behold, to obey *is* better than sacrifice, *and* to hearken than the fat of rams.

At every turn, you are told that you shouldn't have to put up with an inferior product or make-do with something that is less than perfect. So, just dispose of that old car and get a new one. That washer and dryer aren't the latest models, so you better hurry down during the weekend sale and get a new one. Why? Because you deserve it. Really? Really? Well, of course. I mean, you work hard at your job, you have sacrificed for your kids, and you deserve nothing less than the best. And if you carry this logic through, one might conclude that since I should have the very best and not have to make-do with the old vacuum cleaner or microwave, why should I have to make-do with this old, difficult, flaw-ridden marriage? I guess I deserve something better than a spouse who doesn't appreciate me 24/7. I deserve a spouse who is better looking, more attentive, makes more money, and is more masculine or feminine. Life is too short to settle for less. I need to throw away this man or woman and go find the best because, well, I deserve it.

Beginning with Adam and Eve's kids, we see a similar flaw in thinking. Cain and Abel had an issue surrounding their sacrifices to God. Actually, in reality this was probably more of a heart issue. But the bottom line was that God was pleased with Abel's offering, and He was displeased with Cain's. Well, for Cain this just wouldn't do. He felt that he had worked hard and brought an offering like he was supposed to. So, he deserved better. God should be pleased with him too. He didn't see this as his issue to correct, but he saw it as God's issue. Therefore, he would solve this by removing the one with whom God was pleased, then Cain would somehow get what he felt he deserved. As we know from the incident, killing his brother did not even begin to get Cain what he wanted. As a matter of fact, this logic basically ended his role in the story, relegating him to a place of irrelevance.

In Exodus 20, we find that the children of Israel had come to a very significant place in their covenantal journey with God. He was about to give them His laws to live by, which would deepen their special relationship. God had called Moses to come up to Mount Sinai to receive what we know as the Ten

Commandments. Moses spent significant time there with God. But it wasn't long before the people got restless. They were convinced that Moses had died, that God had forsaken them, and that they needed some other kind of spiritual connection. Wanting to please the people as well as to feel more spiritual, Moses' brother Aaron instructed the people to bring their gold and jewelry to him, which he then melted down to fashion a golden calf for the people to worship. Now once again, they felt spiritual. However, as we know, God was displeased and many people died that day.

The Israelites tried to use this very logic. You may recall that the leaders sent 12 spies to check out the land of Canaan. When the spies returned, their reports were mixed. Ten of the spies relayed that the land was full of giants that they could never defeat. They explained that the situation was bleak; they might as well give up this idea of the Promised Land and settle for a trailer park in the swamps. However, the other two spies reported that the land was indeed all that God had promised. It was ready for the taking. All they needed to do was to trust God, and it would be theirs. Well, the people listened to the fears of the ten spies and started looking for doublewides. Their lack of faith displeased God. He responded by telling them that they were obviously not ready to inherit something this lavish, so instead they would have to hang out in the desert for 40 years, Ah, you know, we really didn't consult God about this decision to be scared and not take the land He promised. We didn't seek His will as we should, so we will change our position now and get out of this desert situation and do what we should have done in the first place. Not a good idea. Doubting God and having to hang out in the desert may not have been God's initial desire for you. However, once you made that choice, then He made it pretty clear that waiting four decades for the promise land was now His will. But rather than obey, the Israelites continued to take things into their own hands and rushed in to take the land. What happened? They were soundly defeated and suffered a great loss.

Proverbs 14:12 There is a way which seemeth right unto a man, but the end thereof *are* the ways of death.

In First Samuel 16, we read about the dilemma of King Saul. He went into battle with orders from God through the prophet Samuel instructing him to leave all spoils behind. He was not to take any livestock, nothing. However, Saul disobeyed and brought back stuff from the conquest. As the prophet approached and heard the bleating of sheep, he questioned Saul as to what he had done. Saul responded by saying he only brought back animals so that they could be an offering to God.

Convenience will lead to a conflicted and disjointed journey depending on how far I walk apart from the Lord. It is imperative that we expose the excuses and lies for what they are. It is time to dump the rationalizations that support our conveniences. While God understands divorce, he also understands our marriages, our weaknesses, and even our excuses. He loves us through them, and yet, He calls us to live above the excuses. As believers, it is essential that we walk forward with honesty, stripped of faulty excuses, intent on pursuing God's desires and honoring Him with our choices.

CHAPTER ELEVEN
Saving Your Marriage

I think that this is a great place to start. Reconciliation and restoration are not necessarily the same thing. But I want to emphasize that reconciliation is first and foremost a prerequisite to any hope of restoration. Yet, even when a restoration of the marriage is not possible, perhaps due to a remarriage, reconciliation is always possible. Some people are just looking to get back together. They reason that, If we are together, then we are reconciled and restored. Reconciliation is so much more than that. You may currently find yourself in one of these situations: living under the same roof but occupying different rooms in the house and living in a cold silence; separated and living in different locations; in the process of divorce proceedings, just waiting for the final gavel to fall and give it finality; divorced but aching for it not to be; or divorced and remarried, but continuing to deal with your ex-spouse over everything from finances to custody issues. My warning to you is that some form of reconciliation is possible in all of these situations. If you are hoping to restore a relationship, reconciliation is an absolute necessity.

The first, and probably the most difficult, concept to grasp is that time is a good thing. I know, as you sit in your house alone, worrying about your spouse's activities, wanting to somehow fill the void of your own loneliness, time and waiting do not seem like a good thing. Yet, it is a must! This is an opportunity for you to get emotionally, and perhaps even physically, healthier than you have been in a long time. It is interesting to watch separated couples go through reconciliation. This is where one person is in a place desiring to work on the marriage, while the other is not. Yet, given a little time, that person may come around and be ready to give things another look, only to find that the first partner is no longer interested. It seems that the parties usually cycle through a reconciliation phase with some regularity. If that is the case, then time is important. If you desire reconciliation with your spouse, it is imperative that, whether you are separated or divorced, you not date anyone other than your spouse for two reasons. First, you are probably carrying around emotional baggage with open-heart wounds that do not need to be taken into a new relationship. The other person deserves someone a little more whole, and that is probably not you at the moment. The second reason is that time allows your former mate to cycle back into a reconciliation mindset. If you have already moved on to another relationship then that reconciliation door is probably no longer open to your mate. I want to remind you again that one of your first priorities is to become more emotionally stable and healthy. With appropriate, self-examination, peeling of layers, and rebuilding, it can happen. But it will still take time. There is no substitute. How long will it take? I have been asked that more times than I can count, and I wish there was a standard answer, but there is not. It really does have to do with a multitude of factors. My encouragement is to ask yourself some important questions. Are you stable enough to make a time commitment toward reconciliation? I am not talking a week or two here. Can you make a commitment toward this process for say a year or two or longer? Many feel that they just can't be by themselves, which is a sure sign of psychological instability. Are you willing to learn to be single and content? Until you can truly be okay by yourself, you have more deficits than assets to take into any relationship be that with your spouse or any other person. This is a perfect time to develop good, same-sex friendships. Without them, you will look to opposite-sex relationships to fulfill all of your relationship needs, and that kind of desperation will smother and kill the relationship. You have to ask yourself whether you can learn to make it on your own financially. This can be important in rebuilding your stability. Probably a more difficult question to ask, if you are the one that initiated the divorce proceedings, it is whether you can stop that process and, put it all on hold while you pursue reconciliation? There are many other questions to address regarding how you react to your spouse's friends, your in-laws, and so on. I have just raised a few to get you thinking about the importance of, and the commitment that is needed, to really give reconciliation a shot. It is easy to look at this and think, This is just too hard. I would much rather just find someone else and start again. I would contend that when all is said and done, just starting over really isn't the easier option, but it certainly may look like it right now. We have to remember that reconciliation is a choice. It is a choice against separation and divorce. It is a choice to pursue the type of marital intimacy that God desires for us. Yet, while it is a choice, One of the hardest things to get across to a formerly married single person is that reconciliation is not always an option for the Christian intent on obeying God.

The apostle Paul felt it was vital for Christians to be reconciled to one another. God pleads with us for reconciliation in our relationships.

2 Corinthians 5:18, 19 And all things *are* of God, who hath reconciled us to himself by Jesus Christ, and hath given to us the ministry of reconciliation; To wit, that God was in Christ, reconciling the world unto himself, not imputing their trespasses unto them; and hath committed unto us the word of reconciliation.

The Gospel of Jesus is that reconciliation is possible. God has worked for that throughout our history. He has given Himself to us, time and time again, in the face of mockery, betrayal, and rejection. He continues to pursue us and to pursue reconciliation with us. He models it for us and asks the same of us in our relationships. God did not create marriage for divorce, but for reconciled, intimate, selfless, beautiful relationships. If you are ready to commit yourself to a process of reconciliation, be aware that you are liable to face some of the same things that God faces with us. Even in His perfect plan of redemption and renewal, He was outright rejected, discarded, laughed at, minimized, and treated as unwanted and unneeded. Know that as you pursue reconciliation with your spouse, in all likelihood you will be responded to in some of these same unkind and discounting ways. But remember, this is not a one-shot attempt. It is a commitment to a process that takes time. The sufficiency of God's grace will see you through this.

Reconciliation is possible, it is not easy nor is it automatic. Just because you may desire it doesn't mean that it will come about. You will have to be intentional very intentional. It is easy to say that you want reconciliation, but I would ask, Do you really? Are you willing to sacrifice of yourself, get past your pride, and really do what is necessary to achieve it? If you are currently separated, going through a divorce, contemplating a divorce, or even divorced but hoping to restore the marriage, then I want to suggest some steps that you can take in this endeavor toward reconciliation.

You need to make a commitment to a substantial time frame during which your focus will be on reconciliation with your mate. This is not a time to date or consider other relationships. For those of you who are not divorced, remember that if you are not free to marry, then you are not free to date either. If your time commitment is for a year or two years or whatever other length of time you may decide, you are saying that during this period, you are going to view your focus, your energy, and your efforts through this filter of reconciliation. Are your thoughts, words, and actions in line with your goal to be reconciled? I would even suggest that you begin to journal. Write down what it is you are committing yourself to. Make regular entries about what and how you are doing in your efforts. Keep track of your progress including mistakes and successes.

We live in a society that prides itself on the fact we are tolerant. We are tolerant of other religions, various nationalities, differing lifestyles, and varying sets of moral standards. Ethics have become relative in a post-modern society. Each person decides for him- or herself what is right. This same philosophy has infected the marriage relationship. Millions of people who label themselves as Christians have gone through the tragedy of divorce. It seems that being a Christian has been very little help in sparing them from the pain that a non-Christian would experience. Why is this? Oftentimes it comes down to an inability to accept God's authority. God has given clear instructions regarding marriage, divorce, and reconciliation. We wouldn't expect nonbelievers to follow those instructions. Yet, we would hope that followers of Jesus would submit to His desires for our lives. We would expect God's children to heed His instructions. In order for this to take place, Christians need to remove the word divorce from their vocabulary literally. The use of this word should be stricken from ever being used in a marriage relationship. If you never entertain the idea; if you never discuss that particular possibility; if that option is never available; if you just do not use that word, then of course the potential for that developing is not nearly as great. We should instead replace this word in our vocabulary with the word reconciliation.

In a perfect world, all would be fair. It seems only fair that if I begin to make changes that I need to make, my spouse ought to make changes that she needs to make as well. And she would in a perfect world. However, as you may have noticed in your years of experience, we live in anything but a perfect world. Therefore, the reality is that change begins with one person, and in this case that one person is going to be you. I counseled individuals who want to understand, clarify, and gain insight first. While these can sometimes be helpful, it is important to understand that insight leads to insight not change. Change leads to change. In other words, I have to make a decision to change and then begin to do it, even if I don't fully grasp all of the understanding as to why. You take the lead in doing what you need to do. You don't do it because your spouse is changing too. You do it because it is the best and right thing to do.

Ephesians 4:9-32 (Now that he ascended, what is it but that he also descended first into the lower parts of the earth? He that descended is the same also that ascended up far above all heavens, that he might fill all things.) And he gave some, apostles; and some, prophets; and some, evangelists; and some, pastors and teachers; For the perfecting of the saints, for the work of the ministry, for the edifying of the body of Christ: Till we all come in the unity of the faith, and of the knowledge of the Son of God, unto a perfect man, unto the measure of the stature of the fulness of Christ: That we *henceforth* be no more children, tossed to and fro, and carried about with every wind of doctrine, by the sleight of men, *and* cunning craftiness, whereby they lie in wait to deceive; But speaking the truth in love, may grow up into him in all things, which is the head, *even* Christ: From whom the whole body fitly joined together and compacted by that which every joint supplieth, according to the effectual working in the measure of every part, maketh increase of the body unto the edifying of itself in love. This I say therefore, and testify in the Lord, that ye henceforth walk not as other Gentiles walk, in the vanity of their mind, Having the understanding darkened, being alienated from the life of God through the ignorance that is in them, because of the blindness of their heart: Who being past feeling have given themselves over unto lasciviousness, to work all uncleanness with greediness. But ye have not so learned Christ; If so be that ye have heard him, and have been taught by him, as the truth is in Jesus: That ye put off concerning the former conversation the old man, which is corrupt according to the deceitful lusts; And be renewed in the spirit of your mind; And that ye put on the new man, which after God is created in righteousness and true holiness. Wherefore putting away lying, speak every man truth with his neighbour: for we are members one of another. Be ye angry, and sin not: let not the sun go down upon your wrath: Neither give place to the devil. Let him that stole steal no more: but rather let him labour, working with *his* hands the thing which is good, that he may have to give to him that needeth. Let no corrupt communication proceed out of your mouth, but that which is good to the use of edifying, that it may minister grace unto the hearers. And grieve not the holy Spirit of God, whereby ye are sealed unto the day of redemption. Let all bitterness, and wrath, and anger, and clamour, and evil speaking, be put away from you, with all malice: And be ye kind one to another, tenderhearted, forgiving one another, even as God for Christ's sake hath forgiven you.

Yes, I understand that you feel that your spouse has severely wronged you, and you just can't seem to get past it. But understand that hanging on to that bitterness will keep you stuck and unable to move forward. Paul's instructions are that we get rid of it, we let go of those old resentments, and we extend forgiveness to our spouse just as God has done to us. If you choose to feed the anger and allow it to live in your heart, the bitterness will remain. It is your choice as to what you will do with it.

We are so very good at blaming. We are more comfortable casting blame onto others, circumstances, our past, our upbringing, the failures of our parents, our spouse, our financial situation, our education, our body or face, our social circle, even God. We rationalize. We blame. We repress. We fight against accepting personal responsibility, and in doing so we become tied to our failures and the guilt and shame they drag behind them. We also become tied to the probability of making the same mistakes in the future. During this period of reconciliation, it is imperative that you begin to stop placing blame outside of yourself. This isn't to minimize the wrongs that the other person may have committed. But it is a realization that you can't change or fix them. All you can modify is your own behavior. What have your contributions been to the demise of the relationship? These may be hurtful things that you have done or loving behaviors that you have failed to do. Are you having difficulty finding your failures? Let me ask you this. Are there things that you could have done that would have made the relationships better? Without fail, individuals always answer this question with an affirmative. So, I would encourage you to begin there. As you peel back the layers of your missteps, I can assure you that you will begin to find more and more work that needs to be done. Some fear that if they begin to honestly look at their shortcomings, the search will never end because they know that deep down inside there are many. However, my experience has shown that when people begin to authentically examine their stuff, a weight is lifted and true freedom from emotional oppression begins to take place. As that happens, the positive impact on the relationship can be pleasantly surprising. Take the risk. The fear is unfounded and the results are more than worth the risk.

Philippians 4:6, 7 Be careful for nothing; but in every thing by prayer and supplication with thanksgiving let your requests be made known unto God. And the peace of God, which passeth all understanding, shall keep your hearts and minds through Christ Jesus.

If we will overlay this instruction on our life, we will have taken the first step toward emotional stability. I find emotional overdependence to be a frequent problem for both men and women. I see it early on in the teen years. A girl feels that she has to have a boyfriend or else there is something wrong with her. A boy feels that he is somehow lacking if he doesn't have a girl on his arm. I see individuals who are so dependent upon someone else that they are not complete, and certainly not happy, if they don't have that other person. This is not healthy. We were designed to stand as individuals first and to develop as couples second. This unhealthy need to lean on another has caused some to immediately look for someone else when their spouse leaves. They can't seem to stand on their own two feet. They are not complete and have no identity without someone else attached to them. Again, this is not healthy! If you fit this description, and many will, it is time to take Paul's words to heart and begin to make choices that will allow you to begin to stand on your own, even when it feels awkward and lonely. Let that feeling remind you that you are taking needed healthy steps toward becoming a stable individual.

If an individual says to me, I am going to begin to fix dinner three times a week so that my wife can have a break when she gets home from work, I know that this may really happen. However, if he had simply said that his goal was to be more loving, I would see this as pretty vague with limited chance for success. In that vein of thinking, I want to suggest seven action goals that you might begin to pursue. This is by no means an exhaustive list, but rather one to get you primed.

- Find specific ways in which to show your mate honor and respect.
- Don't criticize your mate.
- Make a list of ways that you can express God's love to your mate. Then begin by picking one of the ways and acting upon it.
- Come up with a list of irritating and annoying things that you do to your mate that you will stop doing. Select one and purposefully avoid doing that behavior.
- Show kindness. Do this with your words as well as with your actions. Make a list of kind acts that you perform and begin to do them.
- Build up your mate instead of tearing him or her down. Remember Paul's words from Ephesians,

Ephesians 5:29 For no man ever yet hated his own flesh; but nourisheth and cherisheth it, even as the Lord the church:

Find specific ways in which to do this.

A commitment to a process of reconciliation is not an easy one or for the faint of heart. However, not only is it one that God asks you to do, but it is one that He will provide you the strength to see through. One of the fruits of the Spirit is self-control. All of the steps that I have outlined require this particular fruit. It is nice to know that God doesn't ask us to do something without giving us the tools and the strength to pull it off. He does not leave us powerless. He has given us the Holy Spirit, and by His comforting, strengthening power, we are able to respond to our spouse in ways that we could never do on our own. As a matter of fact, it is probably for this very reason, doing it on your own, that you find yourself in your current situation. Rest assured. God will provide the resources to enable you to experience a far richer marriage. He will provide you what you need during this process of reconciliation.

CHAPTER TWELVE
Reconciliation

I want to talk more about the subject of reconciliation. I'm more specifically talking about reconciliation with your ex. It is also for those who are divorced and even remarried. Remember, reconciliation is about being friendly again and coming back to a place of harmony. If you have children with your ex-spouse, then you will continue to deal with your ex, in some manner, for years to come, perhaps for the rest of your life. Most ex-relationships are ones of bitterness and hostility. How life-draining that can be. Wouldn't it be much better if it weren't that way? I want to encourage you in a couple of important directions that I think can be helpful when it comes to reconciling with your ex-spouse. Resolve to parent in a manner that is honoring God, your children, your ex-spouse, and yourself. Children are not pawns, trophies, or weapons to be used against your former spouse. Children are a gift and a responsibility from God. Together, you and your ex-spouse must find a way to honestly put your children's needs above your personal hurt. Assume for a minute that your ex-spouse loves your children just as much as you do. Surely, if that is true, the two of you can begin to find a way to parent in a manner that honors all involved. Learn that peace is better than conflict. God calls us to live at peace with each other. I can't begin to tell you how many people that I see who experience physical and emotional dysfunction because they have chosen a lifestyle of conflict and hatred over one of peace. Review the previous eight steps and see how they might apply to you in order for you to experience reconciliation with your ex-spouse. The effort will be worth it.

I believe God is a restorer. Restoration carries with it the concept of bringing something back to its previous condition or its former status. Couples frequently talk about restoration with the idea that they want things returned to the way that they were. However, when we more closely examine the way things were, we often find that they were a mess that had the potential to lead to a gap in the relationship, which they did. The truth of the matter is, couples rarely want things the way that they were; what they actually want is what they dreamed they would have when they got married. They have probably never had that, but would love to have it. I wish I could give you a formula to follow so that all could be restored. However, it is an ongoing process, not a formula.

Yes, trust can be rebuilt, but it must start with a foundation of integrity. It is possible that you will be able to trust your spouse again and be trusted by your spouse, but a pattern of integrity and trustworthiness must come first. If you have not been a person of integrity then you have a challenge ahead of you. It is not easy, but I promise you that change, lasting change, is possible. Trust is essential to restoration.

Many people keep searching for the right person to make them happy. They keep trading one partner in for another in their quest to be happy. Their mistake lies in the fact that happiness is a one-person show. You can't rely on someone else to make you happy. You must first learn to be satisfied with your own life, and then seek to develop a significant relationship by offering your God-given strengths to that relationship.

If a marriage is to be restored to what it was, or to what you both dreamed it would be, it will involve intimacy. Without physical intimacy, it is difficult for spouses to connect emotionally or spiritually. Emotional intimacy develops as intentional and consistent acts of love are built upon a foundation of trust. Spiritual closeness is probably one of the most ignored areas in marriages. It will never happen by itself, but it will be the result of two people intentionally working to develop this area. Structured times of study, authentic sharing of lives, openly bringing your prayer life together before the Lord, and honest communication are all components of spiritual closeness.

Dream out loud, talk, pray, play, honor each other, have fun, and then do it all again. These are important pieces to a restored relationship that achieve what was, and more importantly, what can be.

This is a commonly asked question when one person wants to work on the marriage while the other person doesn't. Certainly, it is much easier when both people come to the table ready to give their all and do what it takes to bring their marriage back to a place of honor. When two people do that, their marriage will most likely be salvaged, restored, and brought to heights unseen before. But what if your spouse has taken his toys and gone home? What if he or she refuses to come to the table and work toward restoration? What do you do? There can be many reasons that this situation exists. It could be that he or she is in the middle of an affair and has no desire to give it up. Most affairs end within six months. If you can wait at the table of reconciliation, there may be an opportunity to get past this. Another possibility is that your spouse doubts the sincerity of your desire and efforts to change. Perhaps he has heard your intentions before, but has not seen any long-term follow through. For whatever reason, you find yourself at the table alone and your spouse won't participate. What do you do? I encourage you to pursue righteousness. God desires that you be in relationship with Him, that you obey His instructions, and that you live to His standard. This can be a challenge, especially when your spouse may be doing the exact opposite. You have to remind yourself that you do not answer to God for your spouse; you answer for you. Do what is right even when he or she doesn't. If you will do that, God will be there for tomorrow, and the next day, and the next.

As you sit at the reconciliation table alone, you will be very tempted to just give up. It would emotionally be much easier, but it will not lead to reconciliation. I promise you that I know what it is like to sit at the table, ready to work, with no one sitting across from you. But I also promise you that, if you will look to your side, you will find the Holy Spirit sitting there with you.

You are not alone. Don't give up.

God has called us to journey with Him and grow each day in our walk. He calls us to do the same in our marriage. If you don't like the way things are in your marriage, ask for what you want, give the other person what they need, and work to improve it. Don't just accept mediocrity.

Romans 8:28 And we know that all things work together for good to them that love God, to them who are the called according to *his* purpose.

Notice that this Scripture doesn't just say that God will make good things happen for you. He says that to those who love Him and have been called according to His purpose. If that statement fits you, then it will be manifested in your actions of obedience, trust, and perseverance, as you rely upon God's strength.

CHAPTER THIRTEEN
The Structure of Divorce

Let's look more into the design of divorce. Jesus clearly indicated in Matthew 5 that when we are married we become one flesh. As Scripture indicates, it is no longer me and her. A husband now loves his wife. This joining together is not a loss of who we are as individual personalities, but it is the creation of a life that didn't exist before. We have taken all that we are our strengths, giftings, the manners in which we do things, the ways that we think and process, our insights and brought them to the mixing bowl. God takes those varied and different, yet complementary, ingredients and makes something new and exciting that did not exist before. Once we are married, we are no longer two but one. We offer to God, as well as others, a partnership, a life that is a brand-new creation. While this may feel somewhat mysterious, I believe it is a concept that God wants us to understand. He wants us to understand that this is something significant, not to be taken lightly. When two people come together, a new life is created. Many times, I have seen individuals view the matter with this kind of weightiness.

However, in our country today, we see kids who get married because they naively believe that another person will fulfill all of their dreams and make them happy. We see cheap assembly-line marriages in places like Las Vegas, where a couple can, whether on a whim or because they are overly intoxicated, get married any time of the day. Have they contemplated the lifelong significance of this new life? Hardly. They have simply done what they felt like doing at the moment. Regardless, a new life is created. This new life is of life-changing, world-impacting significance. It has even been likened to God's relationship with us, which we will discuss in a later chapter. So here we are with this new life. It is not the same as it was. We can even see it in the traditional name change.

You have probably known friends who have gone through a divorce and found yourself having a difficult time thinking of one without the other. When two individuals decide to join their lives together in marriage, they create and become a part of a new life. Now that we understand this idea of a new life, we need to examine the counterpart to that. And that is a new death. When a couple enters into a divorce, they begin the process of death to the relationship, a death to this life. I have spoken with hundreds of people experiencing divorce involving all forms of pain. Men and women will frequently say that a death would be easier to live with and deal with than a divorce, because in a death there is at least some kind of finality and closure that one usually isn't able to experience in a divorce. Actually, divorce is sometimes referred to as a living death for this very reason. I want to use the remainder of this chapter to look at the anatomy of divorce, a detailed examination of what this dying process looks like and entails. It doesn't always look the same. It begins in different ways, proceeds differently, and can end with a variety of ugliness. Some people get sick and die of a disease. Others are killed in an auto accident. Still others are killed in an unexpected tragedy. This is also true of marriages. While this will certainly not be an exhaustive examination, we will look at a few examples of what this death can look like. At this point, I have chosen not to address issues involving sexual or physical abuse or drugs and alcohol, but rather those issues common to most couples. You may see your friends, or even yourself, in these real life depictions.

Chapter Fourteen
Until It Breaks

I want you to think about a rubber band and notice you can stretch it out until it breaks. Most couples that I know have to, at one time or another, address money issues. We need more. We can't pay the bills. We are never able to take a vacation, and on and on. Individuals often come together with extremely different views of how to handle money and some are even frighteningly creative. Without some kind of intervention and change in behavior, this marriage would be in serious trouble. This new life, this body of marriage, was beginning to show early signs of death.

The reasons can vary as to why people are in financial situations. If you are currently facing, or have gone through divorce, it may seem to center on issues of finances, intimacy, expectations, or parenting. However, your situation may look completely different. Perhaps your wounded relationship has to do with unjust criticism, lack of forgiveness, a void of meaningful communication, or broken trust. Regardless of what seems to have led you to this place, the pain is real, and it runs deep. You never stood at the altar thinking that you would be going through such gut-wrenching agony now. In light of your early love and unwavering expressions of commitment, this is absolutely unthinkable. Yet the unthinkable has happened. We created a new life together, one that had not existed before, but that was supposed to last a lifetime. That was certainly your intent, your mate's intent, and God's design. Yet, it is very possible that as you read this, you are staring at the corpse of your created life together, or at the least, a very, very sick body. Regardless of the situations that arose and contributed to where you are, the result is the same: death of the most significant human relationship in your life. It hurts more than anything you could have ever imagined. The loneliness is overwhelming, and you are honestly not sure that you will ever recover. How can someone survive this? You want to scream out so others will grasp the devastation of your searing pain. Yet, you are convinced that no one can understand. Indeed, perhaps no person really can. But without offering trite platitudes, you must know that God sees every tear, hears every cry, and knows every stab of piercing pain that you experience. He doesn't miss a beat and He truly "gets it." Rest assured God understands your divorce completely!

CHAPTER FIFTEEN
What is God's Will?

In any relationship we should find what is God's will. Especially when we are separated or divorced we need to know God's will. God's Will is a very common phrase in Christian circles. Whether we are discussing where we will live, our occupational choice, or the person we are dating, we often do so under the umbrella of what we think God's will is. We talk, we seek counsel, we pray, and we think all in an effort to discern this seemingly mysterious, and somewhat subtle, piece of information. If we could just determine this, all would be well or so we think. Certainly there are subjects where God's will seems less than crystal clear or perhaps comes with many options. Thus, we include a variety of pieces in an effort to best understand what He would want. However, on this particular subject matter marriage and divorce we can sit back and relax. We don't have to go through any mental gyrations in order to know God's will. He has made it relatively simple and pretty clear for us. So, let's examine this together.

1 Samuel 15:22 And Samuel said, Hath the LORD *as great* delight in burnt offerings and sacrifices, as in obeying the voice of the LORD? Behold, to obey *is* better than sacrifice, *and* to hearken than the fat of rams.

John 14:23 Jesus answered and said unto him, If a man love me, he will keep my words: and my Father will love him, and we will come unto him, and make our abode with him.

We could look at a number of other Scriptures that teach that God desires we obey Him. Certainly, we try to rationalize how our disobedience will make sense in our particular situation, because it is for a good cause, and somehow the ends will justify the means. But I don't think that we will find that God necessarily takes this same view. Remember when Ananias and Sapphira decided to donate a sizeable gift to the early church. They sold a piece of property and apparently wanted to donate some of the proceeds and keep some of them as well. While they were certainly free to do this, what they weren't free to do was to lie to the church about it. Rather than just say Hey we sold some land and want to donate part of the money, they chose to say they were donating all of the profit to the church. What happened when they came into the church and attempted to pull off this scheme? God took their lives.

Acts 5:1-11 But a certain man named Ananias, with Sapphira his wife, sold a possession, And kept back *part* of the price, his wife also being privy *to it,* and brought a certain part, and laid *it* at the apostles' feet. But Peter said,

Ananias, why hath Satan filled thine heart to lie to the Holy Ghost, and to keep back *part* of the price of the land? Whiles it remained, was it not thine own? and after it was sold, was it not in thine own power? why hast thou conceived this thing in thine heart? thou hast not lied unto men, but unto God. And Ananias hearing these words fell down, and gave up the ghost: and great fear came on all them that heard these things. And the young men arose, wound him up, and carried *him* out, and buried *him*. And it was about the space of three hours after, when his wife, not knowing what was done, came in. And Peter answered unto her, Tell me whether ye sold the land for so much? And she said, Yea, for so much. Then Peter said unto her, How is it that ye have agreed together to tempt the Spirit of the Lord? behold, the feet of them which have buried thy husband *are* at the door, and shall carry thee out. Then fell she down straightway at his feet, and yielded up the ghost: and the young men came in, and found her dead, and, carrying *her* forth, buried *her* by her husband. And great fear came upon all the church, and upon as many as heard these things.

Why was lying such a big deal when they were still doing a good thing? God didn't want deception and didn't need their money. What He wants is honesty and obedience. Or what about Uzzah? *Who?* Uzzah: the man who seemed to have the best of intentions to protect God's stuff. In First Chronicles 13, we read about what happened when King David decided to have the ark of the Covenant moved. The Israelites were assembled and the priests had their assigned duties about how the ark was to be transported. By God's decree, only certain people were allowed to touch the ark. They moved the ark of God from Abinadab's house on a new cart, with Uzzah and Ahio guiding it. David and all the Israelites were celebrating with all their might before God, with songs and with harps, lyres, tambourines, cymbals and trumpets. When they came to the threshing floor of Kidon, Uzzah reached out his hand to steady the ark, because the oxen stumbled. The Lord's anger burned against Uzzah, and he struck him down because he had put his hand on the ark. So He died before God.

1 Chronicles 13:7-10 And they carried the ark of God in a new cart out of the house of Abinadab: and Uzza and Ahio drave the cart. And David and all Israel played before God with all *their* might, and with singing, and with harps, and with psalteries, and with timbrels, and with cymbals, and with trumpets. And when they came unto the threshingfloor of Chidon, Uzza put forth his hand to hold the ark; for the oxen stumbled. And the anger of the LORD was kindled against Uzza, and he smote him, because he put his hand to the ark: and there he died before God.

It is easy for us to look at this passage and find ourselves feeling a bit angry. If you read on in the story, you would find that King David even became angry. Again, we rationalize that Uzzah was doing a good thing. Didn't God understand that? What was He thinking? But you have to remember the overriding principle. It is not that God doesn't appreciate a person's sacrificial efforts in life, but above and beyond that, He desires obedience more than sacrifice. His desire was that Uzzah obey what he knew to be right, not to take it upon himself to re-decide whether or not God really meant what He said. Do you think that God, the Creator of all that is, was capable of taking care of the unstable cart? Sure He was. But we often act as though God is incapable and ineffective, and that if we don't step in and act, even if it is different from what God has said, then somehow God's Kingdom will crumble. Is our God that small, or is it just that our egos and sense of self are that over-inflated? Matthew 5:48 states that we are to be perfect. Perhaps a better translation might be complete or mature just as God is. Our desire should be to be mature and complete in our obedience to God. Our desire should be to be more and more like God.

I am convinced the most effective remedy is spiritual renewal on the part of one or the other or both. Someone has to say, I will obey God. I will do what He tells me to do in His Word. What does God desire? He desires that I obey Him and do whatever He tells me in His Word to do!

CHAPTER SIXTEEN
God Honors Obedience

One thing I'm known for from those closest to me is my radical obedience. If God says do this or that I do it. I want to briefly look at three individuals and how they chose to obey God even in the face of seemingly impossible circumstances. They could have easily said, Wait a minute! My very life is on the line here, and God's plan appears to have flaws and weaknesses. I had better do this my way instead. But they didn't. Let's see what happened.

Joseph, the favored son of Jacob, had more than his share of challenging times. You may remember the story of how his father Jacob gave Joseph a beautiful coat of many colors or one that was richly ornamented. His brothers were quite jealous, contemplated killing him, and ultimately sold him into slavery in Egypt. Once in Egypt, a man named Potiphar, the captain of the guard, purchased him. Potiphar realized that Joseph was different, that the Lord was with him, and that he could be trusted. As a result, Joseph was placed in charges of Potiphar's entire household, which in turn led to success and blessings for

Potiphar. All was going well, until Potiphar left town and his wife began to proposition Joseph. Being the man of principle and integrity that Joseph was, he consistently refused her seductive invitations and eventually was forced to flee the premises. Good for Joseph! He didn't falter but was obedient and God blessed him. One would hope so, but that is not exactly what happened at least not immediately. Potiphar's wife lied about what happened and Joseph was thrown into the King's prison. Joseph never wavered. He didn't obey because of what it would get him or because it would make him happy. He obeyed because it was the right thing to do and because it would please God. Joseph was soon given a leadership position in the prison, was called up to interpret a dream for the king, and ultimately became the king's number two man. But as cool as Joseph's vindication is, it is not the reason that Joseph obeyed. He was content to obey whether or not he ever saw daylight out of prison. He was aware that the story was not about him, but about God. This is a difficult lesson for us to learn, but it is essential.

Gideon was a man chosen by God to lead Israel during a period of time as described in the Book of Judges. Gideon was given the task of leading Israel into battle against the Midianites. Gideon was a bit nervous and had been seeking signs of assurance from the Lord to make sure that God was really going to take care of him. Gideon was feeling pretty good because he had gathered the army of Israel together and it consisted of over 30,000 men. This gave Gideon confidence that they might experience some success.

Judges 7:2, 3 And the LORD said unto Gideon, The people that *are* with thee *are* too many for me to give the Midianites into their hands, lest Israel vaunt themselves against me, saying, Mine own hand hath saved me. Now therefore go to, proclaim in the ears of the people, saying, Whosoever *is* fearful and afraid, let him return and depart early from mount Gilead. And there returned of the people twenty and two thousand; and there remained ten thousand.

Gideon was in a state of shock while he worked on a new game plan of how he would pull off this battle with only 10,000 men. But just as he began to strategize with his war advisors,

Judges 7:4 And the LORD said unto Gideon, The people *are* yet *too* many; bring them down unto the water, and I will try them for thee there: and it shall be, *that* of whom I say unto thee, This shall go with thee, the same shall go with thee; and of whomsoever I say unto thee, This shall not go with thee, the same shall not go.

The Lord told Gideon that He would sift through them for Gideon. I can imagine that Gideon was thinking Sift through them? Are you kidding me? I need all of them that I can keep! Yet, Gideon did as the Lord commanded, went through the process down by the water, and left with a mere 300 men. He only had 300 men to attack an entire army! This was not looking good. But God had a plan. All that Gideon had to do was obey and follow it, whether he understood it or not, whether it made sense or not, whether it seemed foolish or reasonable; Gideon just needed to be obedient. If he would be willing to do that, the outcome might be surprising. While you can read the incredible account in Judges 7, just be assured that Gideon did obey. He allowed God to come up with the plan for the group of 300, and the result was an amazing rout of the Midianites.

Daniel was part of a group of royalty and nobility that King Nebuchadnezzar brought in for training after he took over Jerusalem. The king considered Daniel and three of his friends to be the best and brightest when it came to wisdom and understanding. Daniel was called upon more than once to interpret dreams for the king and was later placed in a position of prestige and power by the king. Nebuchadnezzar's son Belshazzar succeeded him as king, followed by King Darius. King Darius was also more than impressed with Daniel's wisdom and integrity. Darius planned to elevate him to a position over the other administrators, which led to a conspiracy by those who were jealous of Daniel. This wicked group of men appealed to the king's vanity and persuaded him to issue an edict that for 30 days all of the people were only allowed to pray to the king. Anyone who violated this order would be thrown into the lion's den. When Daniel heard about this he was disturbed. When you think about it, it would have been quite easy for Daniel to rationalize a behavior that would have kept him out of trouble, at least with Darius. He certainly could have reasoned that God had placed him in this powerful position of influence. It was important that he remain there in order to spread God's influence among the leadership and the people. God needed him there. Besides, he knew that the king didn't have God's power and couldn't answer prayer. So, what harm could be done by just going through the motions? He could humor the king and therefore keep his position, not to mention, his life. Sounds like a feasible plan. But this isn't what Daniel chose to do. Daniel was intent on obeying God. Would it be a good thing for Daniel's influence in the kingdom to continue? Perhaps. But it is an even better thing to obey the Creator of the Universe. He can then deal with Darius and Daniel's position of power if He chooses to. If you have read the story, then you know that the king was quite distressed when he heard about Daniel praying to God. He wasn't distressed because of what Daniel did; rather he was upset because he knew he had to adhere to his own decree and throw Daniel to the lions. Try as he did to find an escape clause, King Darius could not, and he placed Daniel in the den. I find it interesting that we don't see Daniel crying, upset, pleading for his life, worried about his loss of influence, or any other number of things that we might find ourselves resorting to. We find just the opposite. Daniel was at peace and accepted his fate. All the while, the king was stressed, couldn't sleep, and worried all night about Daniel's welfare. So, what happened? The next morning the king found Daniel alive and well because God had sent an angel to protect him. Now we can't always assume that obedience will prevent us from being eaten by the lions in our life. But we can know that our obedience to what God desires thoroughly honors and pleases Him. Do you really think that if Daniel had quit praying to God, and given lip service to the king, that God would have continued to use him in a powerful way in the King Darius' kingdom? I sincerely believe that we would have seen just the opposite.

Matthew 10:39 He that findeth his life shall lose it: and he that loseth his life for my sake shall find it.

Had Daniel hung on to his life of power and made that his priority, he would have certainly lost it all. However, because he was willing to give up all that he had in order to please God, life was granted to him. The fullness of life that is afforded because of obedience far outweighs any seeming temporary gains achieved by our rationalized disobedience.

God desires obedience, and we examined some of the ramifications of that. It is important that you make and carry out your decisions from a point of conviction and not convenience. This is such a critical concept that I want to say it again and perhaps a little louder. In other words, study to see exactly what God says and allow that alone to determine what you do. Too many times, I see individuals enter the discussion with preconceived ideas and desires. They know what they want to do before the discussion even begins. So, they work diligently to create an intellectual scaffolding to support their preconceived desires. This is what I call a decision that comes from convenience. People do mental and intellectual gymnastics to create an argument, to build a defense, for what they want, regardless of the facts. This is being intellectually dishonest with yourself and with God. Set your course of action based upon conviction that comes from understanding God's Word.

God's plan is clear, but it makes people uncomfortable. Why? God's plan is what *God* wants. When things are difficult or hard, God's plan is not what we want. In our limited and twisted wisdom, we want things that are easy, things that make us happy, things that please us, and so on. It is sad to say, but true. We are frequently more interested in what will please us than we are with what will please God. Why do our behaviors indicate that we don't truly believe that God knows what He is doing? We think that He doesn't get it or is asleep, because we take matters into our own hands. God knows what He designed, how we are meant to work, what is best for us, and overall He knows what He is doing! What a concept! God's will is not that we divorce, but that we love, forgive, reconcile, and redeem our marriages in order to honor Him. We also receive an amazing by-product of achieving satisfaction ourselves. We already know it is God's will for marriages to be restored, though God respects human freedom. I cannot discuss and cover every conceivable conflict and dysfunction that may appear in your marriage. What I can say is what God states clearly: You are to leave your parents, be completely committed to your spouse, build a united and intimate marriage that lasts for the rest of your life, and honor God's will, your commitment to your spouse, and the very vows that you offered. This is God's will. God's will is not confused or conflicted, but quite clear!

Chapter Seventeen
Life is Short

We go through life thinking we always have plenty of time. What we have is worth fighting for because if we don't then we find out we will have many regrets. There are two basic views of life. Either we see life as an end in itself or as a means to an end. If it is an end in itself, then this is all there is. I have one shot, and I had better enjoy it all I can while it lasts, because when my time is up, we're done. There is nothing else. This is it. This view will certainly impact decisions that we make about marriage and divorce. With this mind-set, divorce becomes a very rational option. If I am miserable or unhappy, I must get out because life is too short to live this way. I am not going to live like this. I am going to throw away this negative baggage and move on in pursuit of a fulfilling life. However, if my perspective is that God is here and in complete control, then life is a blip on the radar screen. By that I mean that this life is but a dot on a range of eternity. I realize that the end, the goal, is spending all of time in the presence of God. That relationship is my goal and where my efforts are directed. How does my marriage fit into this? There are many ways, but I will just mention a few. Marriage provides me a partner with whom to travel and serve. Marriage allows God to work through another human to mold, shape, and grow me in His image. If you are married, then you know, as much as you may hate it, your spouse knows you and your faults unlike anyone else, except God. I truly believe that God can use our mate to bring out our garbage, which in turn allows us to see it, own it, address it, and get rid of it. God can use our mates to help us grow into becoming more like Him. Marriage honors God, and it honors people. I have heard people complain about various aspects of their jobs. I can choose to live for the moment or for what comes next. However, if I look closely, I might find that how I choose to deal with this moment will impact my relationships in eternity as well as the quality of this moment. Please don't misunderstand me and think that this life is irrelevant, or that I am minimizing the difficulties of it. Believe me; I know better than that. It is significant and can even seem all-consuming. I would like to be happy and enjoy this moment called life. All I am saying is that if my goal is God's purposes for all of eternity, my relationship with Him will be intimate, and my moment will be meaningful, very possibly satisfying, and even happy at times. However, if my focus is the moment and my happiness now, I will likely be very disappointed, unfulfilled, and anything but happy. Yet, when I am in the middle of a seemingly oppressive relationship, an unsatisfying marriage, a downright miserable and depressive life, even the moment can seem like more than I want to handle. How am I to begin to look beyond the moment to see God's bigger picture?

2 Corinthians 12:9, 10 And he said unto me, My grace is sufficient for thee: for my strength is made perfect in weakness. Most gladly therefore will I rather glory in my

infirmities, that the power of Christ may rest upon me. Therefore I take pleasure in infirmities, in reproaches, in necessities, in persecutions, in distresses for Christ's sake: for when I am weak, then am I strong.

Does it sound like Paul is focused on the moment? Not at all. Does that sound like your marriage? Have there been hardships, be they financial or otherwise? Sure there have. Do you get insulted? Paul is saying that if I have an eternity perspective instead of a blip perspective, then all of these things are mere opportunities to grow and become more complete like God. God's grace is sufficient. It is all we need. In our weakness, God's power is made complete. If we choose to live for self and personal happiness, we are free to do so, but let's not continue to say that Jesus Christ is Lord and misrepresent His name and image to others. If we choose to value our subjective experience above the written Word of God, then let's just say so and not claim that the Bible has authority in our lives. If we believe that marriage is a contract rather than a covenant, then let's act accordingly and not perform the ceremony as though it were a covenant before God using covenant language such as until death do us part and other such phrases which are really not consistent with a contract belief.

Chapter Eighteen
Love God

No matter what you go through you have to keep the love for God in your midst. When we fail to love each other, we have failed in our love for God. We must confess the failures of the marriage to God. If we followed God's expressed will regarding marriage instead of diligently looking for loopholes? If we said, I will not try to construct an argument for what I want, but I will act upon God's conviction in my life. If I took the first step and said, I am going to obey God and do His will pure and simple. We have established in scripture that God approves the practice of marriage. It is His appointed way for the entire human race, including those who have sinned against it in the past. We have established also that God forbids the practice of marriage splitting apart. In the viewpoint we have set forth here, it is right to be in a marriage and wrong to sin against a marriage. This is precisely in line with the fundamental facts of scripture. If it were to be accepted by all, the end result would be a total annihilation of divorce, for all who have done it would repent and resolve never to do so again, and all who plan to divorce would change their minds and determine not to do it. It might not be possible to prevent in some cases because the other party in the marriage may be unwilling. But if all parties accepted the viewpoint set forth here, divorce would be eradicated. We would have no divorces because they would have been erased in forgiveness. No future divorces would be coming up, because the minds so intending would have been changed. This would be an amazing consequence of actively doing God's will!

Chapter Nineteen
Divorce's Impact

One thing most don't realize is that divorce has great impact on more than just the bride and groom that lasts for years. The negative impact of divorce runs the range from issues of health to those of finances. Let's briefly touch on a few of the more common ones and look at some things that we have learned.

- Divorce has been shown to contribute to health problems for many of the individuals involved. It led the authors of a book for medical students to write: It is wiser to improve marriage rather than dissolve it, and physicians should encourage marital therapy for troubled marriages.
- Chronic loneliness, social isolation, and the sudden loss of love have been identified as significant contributors to illness and premature death. While on the other hand, physical health is actually enhanced by an intimate relationship in marriage.
- Emotional loneliness springs from the need for intimacy with a spouse or a best friend. A person who is emotionally lonely feels that there is no one he can absolutely count on. Symptoms include

feelings of tension, vigilance against possible threat, restlessness, loss of appetite, an inability to fall asleep, and a pervasive low-level anxiety.

- Working to avoid loneliness can become a monumental relentless task. Yet, another paints the picture accurately when he states, You need to know that divorce leads to loneliness.
- Married individuals are more productive employees.
- Significantly decreased standard of living is frequently apparent in single-parent households.
- The carnage is never over for anyone completely.
- People wonder if being a Christian makes any difference.
- It produces so much pain and damage to the people involved that it does anything but demonstrate God's glory.
- Families are broken up for generations to come.
- Divorce places families in a state of confusion and insecurity.
- Children's loyalties are torn between the two people they love the most. Divorce is the ripping apart of a couple and a family that was never designed to be taken apart. It doesn't affect everyone the same. For some, the consequences may seem minimal, while for others they feel suffocating. But for the most part, if you have been in the middle of it, or journeyed with a friend through it, you know the pain that feels like it could stop life. And if you know that pain, you have a glimpse of what contributes to God's statement, "I hate divorce."

The apostle Paul writes in First Corinthians 7 and reiterates Jesus' words that we are not to divorce. In his discussion of marriage, divorce, and unbelievers who leave a marriage, he states that God has called us to live in peace. We oftentimes would like to force the other person to do the right thing. Yet, we find this technique to be quite unsuccessful. Therefore, Paul is saying, Do what you can, but you can't force anyone to do anything. So, even in these situations, live a life of peace. Yet, divorce typically leads to increased conflict, negative emotions, increased stress, and anything but peace. Following a divorce, spouses frequently assume, or at least hope, that the other person will just fade into the sunset, leave them alone, and be out of his or her life. Yet, this is rarely the case. You may be appalled at how your ex-spouse continues to come at you, attacking at every opportunity. If you have children, you will have little choice but to continue to talk with your ex-spouse. You have to schedule visitations, address vacations and holidays, deal with doctor's appointments, soccer games, and any number of other circumstances. If anything goes wrong while you have the children in your custody, then you may hear accusations of incompetence and irresponsibility. The sad truth is that if you decided to divorce your mate, you will need a lawyer and you will need a judge. Most people cannot make the important decisions necessary without their help. You will be paying lawyers by the hour, so it is in their best interests to prolong the proceedings. They have no real incentive to do their job quickly or expeditiously. The judges, on the other hand, are hard-pressed for time, and your case is not likely to be given the time needed to make a fair and prudent or wise decision. The judges may also be bitter, sick and tired of hearing two people cut each other to pieces with words. If you or your spouse has remarried, then there are issues of a new spouse and perhaps stepchildren as well. Parents are frequently more closely knit to their children than they are to their new spouse's children. Some spouses complain when stepchildren come to the house because he or she is treated almost as if he or she didn't exist and he or she feels completely left out. As much as people may want to be inclusive, people rarely feel the same way about another's children as they do their own. I fully realize that there are probably some who feel better divorced or remarried, but I assure you that the vast majority don't, and studies support this statement.

If you have, or are, contemplating divorce, what you have read may feel overly harsh, bleak, and downright overwhelming and even legalistic. I know they seem hard, but it is essential that I speak truth to you in this area. It is essential that you know. Why does God so clearly state that He hates divorce? For all of the reasons listed above and many more. God is in the business of redeeming and restoring lives, not in destroying them. Yet, destroying is exactly what divorce does to lives, relationships, churches, and communities. This is why Jesus says, Let no man separate what God has joined. God understands, more than anyone, the heartbreaking pain of divorce. And even in the face of blatant unfaithfulness, God still desires restoration. While God divorced Israel, He still desired for her return. He said that if she would return, "I will not be angry forever." God understands divorce, and it is because He understands it so well that He says, I hate it. Stop this unfaithfulness. It is unfaithfulness to your spouse, your children, and to Me. Stop it!

Praise God that He is full of grace. He knows that we regularly learn needed lessons only after we have destroyed something, and it is often beyond repair. Yet, God still loves us and still redeems us. So, what does God say to those of us in this situation? Borrowing from the spirit of several passages, I believe God would say something to us like this: If you are still married, then take the necessary steps to begin to redeem that marriage. Be the husband or wife that you have been called to be especially in and during difficult times. If you are divorced, and neither you or your spouse is remarried, be patient, wait, and seek the restoration of your marriage. This is honoring to me. If you are divorced and are remarried, then become the best husband or wife that you can be to your spouse. Love this spouse with the intentionality that you should have the first time around but failed to do. I hate divorce! Redeem this marriage so that no one experiences another divorce. I have given you My Spirit to lead and fill your every need. I will give you what you need to be the spouse that I have called you to be. Therefore, honor Me in this marriage. Things I discuss in later chapters will help you in your pursuit of this. By sharing facts, statistics, and Scriptures with you, please know that I do not do so from a high and separated, lofty tower. I do so recognizing your pain of possible betrayal, abuse, or any other number of emotions that push us toward divorce. Remember, I have been there. More importantly, God has been there. All of the pain and brokenness are wrapped in, and around, these truths. When our marriages seem the bleakest, remember that God's Word and eternal truths were given for these very times. In our darkest days, let us acknowledge that He knows what He is talking about and honor that with our choices. If we do, His blessings in our marriage and relationships just might surprise us.

CHAPTER TWENTY
What to do?

Love is a choice, I can love my spouse in spite of my feelings. Think about when Jesus taught us to love our enemies. We certainly don't have good feelings toward our enemies, but we can love them anyway. Sometimes you may see your husband or wife as the enemy. You may wonder what you should do when your spouse says that he or she hates you. Jesus teaches us to love him or her in return. In order to do this, we have to put the other person's interests above our own. I know that this can be difficult, especially when everything that you see in the other person makes you want to jump out of your skin. You may need to spend some time looking for the traits or assets that this person has to offer. I know you may think there aren't any. But at one time there certainly were, and as buried as they may be in him or her, they still probably exist. Take some time to rediscover them. Perhaps your feelings are non-existent because your spouse has wronged you.

Most people assume that spending more time together will be the logical result of feeling better about each other. Therefore, they wait for the hostile feelings to be replaced by positive feelings before doing those things that once gave them joy. However, the reverse appears to be true: when couples engage in pleasant activities together, it triggers pleasant feelings, which in turn breed a cooperative spirit.

Whether you feel this way right at this moment or not, there has probably been a time in your life when you did. It might have been in relation to a friend, a sibling, or a spouse. You may have felt that loving someone was just too difficult. Their abrasive edges, their mean spiritedness, their callous insensitivity was just too much. Surely God doesn't expect me to aim my loving behavior gun at them. It is too hard. It seems impossible. Even the disciples struggled with understanding this during their days with Jesus. You may remember that after Jesus corrected the Pharisees' understanding of the durability of marriage in Matthew 19, the disciples responded with,

Matthew 19:10 His disciples say unto him, If the case of the man be so with *his* wife, it is not good to marry.

They also perceived this as a task that was just too tough. Yet, we have to remember that anything God has commanded is not beyond our ability. Would He ask of us what is not possible? Of course not. He knows our weaknesses and our seemingly impossible challenges. But the coolest thing is that God supplies us with the strength to do what He asks. He knows every marital obstacle before we hit it. He is aware of the rollercoaster of emotions that we will experience. He desires for our relationship to be full of depth and intimacy, and He recognizes that this doesn't come without our working through the most difficult of times. While He expects us to do that, He gives us His grace and strength necessary that comes through the Holy Spirit. His strength is bottomless if we will just go to the well and drink from it. Learning to rely on His enduring power as we love our spouse does not mean that we are to just be a door mat and allow our spouse to walk all over us. Many people are healed when someone loves them enough to stand up to their inappropriate actions. It is true that God loves us unconditionally, but it is not true that His approach is the same whether we obey or disobey His commands. We do not receive God's blessing unless we are willing to live responsibly. We cannot have the benefits of a warm, loving relationship unless we are willing to be responsible in our own behavior with our spouses.

Chapter Twenty One
Where is Your Treasure

Matthew 6:21 For where your treasure is, there will your heart be also.

What He is saying is that what we place value upon is where our feelings will be. Whether that is in our finances, our business, our boat, or our golf game. Where we invest our time and energies what we treasure is where our heart or feelings will be. This is just as true in our relationship with our spouse. If this is where we spend our creative energies and place our primary focus, we will be amazed at the outcomes. If I treasure my spouse, my loving feelings about him or her will begin to develop accordingly. We live in a generation where people are more concerned about their rights than they are commitment.

We need to keep our focus on ourselves. I am sure that most of us have focused our expectations on our spouse and worked to change them into what we think they should be. My question is, how well has that worked? And if we keep doing the same old thing, it will continue to not work. We need to focus on our own shortcomings and learn to love as God has instructed us to do, regardless of what our spouse does. Only then can we give our marriage the opportunity to experience genuine transformation. When we begin to pursue this, we create a place of safety and security in our marriage. Every enduring marriage involves an unconditional commitment to an imperfect person.

Chapter Twenty Two
Cultivating Strong Marriages

Our marriages respond in a certain manner. If we take the time to nurture it will grow. If we neglect it will die.

Understanding God's concept of love is critical to our understanding of life. God's love for us demonstrates what love is to be about: His for us, ours for Him, and ours for each other. I want to attempt to summarize God's love in a concise and portable form in other words a useable form that you can carry with you daily. First of all, love is not something that happens *to* us, that is out of our control. It is something that is very much in our control, and we choose it. Second, as taught in First Corinthians 13, love is not a tingly feeling but an intentional action and behavior. If we will do the action consistently, with time the feelings will follow. Third, when it seems too taxing to do, we find that God supplies the ability. With Jesus' love at the heart of who we are, we can do it. Fourth, love breaks down strongholds. Where we invest ourselves, what we make important, our heart will deem as a priority and our feelings will match that. Finally, the love God teaches us to have is an unconditional love. I am committed to loving my spouse (even when he or she is unlovable), just as God wants him or her to be committed to loving us. There are no exit clauses to unconditional love. Love just is, and it is unending. Are you up for redefining your love for your spouse? If you are, it can revolutionize and revitalize your life.

Chapter Twenty Three
Divorce Can Limit Our Potential

Rules and regulations seem to be a necessary evil. Yet, in many cases, even as much as we hate them, we know that they are there for our protection and welfare. Not only are we surprised, but we are in disbelief that someone went so far as to impose consequences for our violation. From the very beginning in The Garden of Eden, Adam and Eve wanted to pass blame and avoid responsibility for their actions. So, I suppose that we come by it quite naturally. If we could get our heads around the fact that consequences are connected to behavior, we might be able to make some changes. It is pretty clear that if I rob a bank, I will go to jail. But you have to understand that our seeming inability to get this is exactly the reason that we are surprised by repercussions to our actions. We have occasionally seen men and women go to prison for some terrible crime and then find Jesus. While I am certainly not questioning the sincerity of their repentance, I want to point out that, even if they are truly remorseful for their actions and even receive forgiveness from the victim and from God, they still have to serve their time. Being sorry doesn't remove the sentence. I may truly regret the fact that I hurriedly walked too close to the edge of a cliff and fell off. I may desperately wish that I had walked slower and would certainly do it differently given another chance. I have learned my lesson. Yet, while that is all well and good—my leg is still broken and will still take weeks to heal. The bottom line is this disobedience often results in unwanted consequences. So, why do I elaborate on all of this? Because thee are often repercussions to divorce that we never considered until we were on the other side saying oops! when it was too late. God is full of grace and forgiveness, and there are absolutes in what God expects and disobeying His instruction will have lifelong implications.

1 Peter 5:8 Be sober, be vigilant; because your adversary the devil, as a roaring lion, walketh about, seeking whom he may devour:

Satan is no respecter of persons he will take down anyone! If the enemy can kill your marriage he can stop the unified potential of you and your spouse.

It is important that we understand what disobedience and divorce do to our relationships with God, our family, and those around us First, when we make decisions that are in contradiction to God's expressed will, He is displeased. This is not unlike what we experience with our children. We love them to pieces and would do anything for them. Yet, when they disobey us, when they do the exact opposite of what we requested of them, two things happen. First we are disappointed and grieved. Second, we don't trust them and are hesitant to rely on them to do future things that we ask. We may even remove privileges and responsibilities from them. This is exactly what God does. He doesn't love us any less; we are not any less His children. But He can't trust us and may have to remove us from positions of influence until He can trust us. Our response to our sin will determine whether we will be trustworthy again or not. Once we have distanced ourselves from closeness with God, we do the same thing with those whom we love. We made lifelong vows of love and commitment to a person whom we are now divorcing. We have brought children into a home that should have been permanent for them, but is now shattered, uncertain, and fraught with fear of the unknown. How will our children view us? Can they really trust that we love them when we place our desires ahead of their welfare?

1 Timothy 3:4, 5 One that ruleth well his own house, having his children in subjection with all gravity; (For if a man know not how to rule his own house, how shall he take care of the church of God?)

And believe me, making decisions that will lead to breaking vows with my spouse through a divorce certainly indicate that I have some issues in managing my own family. How then can I lead in God's Church? That is a significant question that hopefully leads me to wrestle with my issues and myself. We often think that we can just divorce our spouse and that this decision will be isolated from the rest of our lives. However, this is certainly not the case. This decision to break faith with my spouse is pervasive and will seep into every area of my life. It builds walls and damages my intimacy with God. It creates mistrust with my children. They will wonder if I will really be there and if they can trust what I say. It creates doubt among my friends. They will question if I bring dependability to the table, and whether they want me speaking into their lives. It brings overwhelming credibility issues to the forefront in any place where I might be in a position of influence whether that is church or work. My choice to divorce will impact every relationship in my life. With much work, these relationships can be rebuilt. It is critical to understand that, while they will never be the same, they can be healthy once again.

We don't always know all of the details and have all of the insight that God does. We don't always see the loss of credibility among friends, the damage to relationships with children, and so on. Also, keep in mind that as I speak of consequences, for our purposes, I am speaking primarily about consequences as they relate to positions of leadership, especially within the Church, and our ability to have widespread positive impact on people's lives. You may find yourself resisting this idea simply because you don't like it. If that is the case, I understand. I don't like it either. But the longer I observe the lives and ministries of others, the more convinced I am that it is true. As I have been willing to repent, submit in obedience to God, and steadfastly work for authenticity and integrity, God has redeemed my life.

Yes, the Lord has plans for us from the very beginning of our lives, plans that we frequently usurp and make shambles of. I have an amazing ability to take God's plans for me and rework them and fit them into the shape of what I want. Inevitably when I do that, the result is chaos. Do I believe that God may have had plans for me in areas of ministry very different from what I am now doing? I believe that is very possible. Those plans were scrapped, because I made choices that were incompatible with God's purpose and plans for my life. Those opportunities, in their original form, are gone. But again, because of God's grace, if I will humbly and truly submit my heart at His feet, He will redeem my life. He has not abandoned the work of His hands. The Lord will indeed fulfill His purpose in me.

Chapter Twenty Four

My Story and Divorce Transition

It is amazing what people will do in the name of love. I don't know that I can think of a word in our language that is more misused, misunderstood, taken for granted, and yet invoked as much as love. My hope is that, by the end of this chapter, we will have a much clearer understanding of what love is actually all about.

The following is a list of words that a recent class came up with to describe love.

- Commitment
- Unconditional
- Kindness
- Makes me laugh
- Trust
- Patience
- Dependable
- Loyalty

- Sacrifice
- Thoughtful
- Romantic
- Passionate
- Mutual Respect
- Support
- Encouragement
- Forgiveness
- Eternal
- Bonding
- Mercy
- Giving
- Receiving
- Compromise
- Acceptance
- Unfailing
- Adoring
- Exciting

As you can see, these words are all over the board. Depending on a person's background and experiences, different words resonate for different people. But do any of these words singularly capture the concept of love? At one time or another, most of us have fallen in love, we have also probably made the mistake of thinking that this was the same thing as loving someone. As a result, we often use love and falling in love interchangeably. Yet, they are very different. Actually, I personally feel that this idea of falling in love has created a great deal of confusion and done us a huge disservice. Falling in love implies that something just happened to me. It was completely out of my control, and I was just swept away by it.

We think of it when we discuss the virtues of love, and we often include it as a part of many wedding ceremonies. While it frames nicely and looks good hanging on our wall, I wonder if we really know the significance of what these words convey. Just prior to First Corinthians 13, Paul discussed the importance of the various parts of the body that we call the Church, and the various spiritual gifts that help to complete the functioning of that body. He concludes Chapter 12 by encouraging believers to desire the gifts, especially the greatest gift, which is love. He begins Chapter 13 by emphasizing that agape love—the highest form of love is essential. It doesn't matter what other gifts I have, what great works I can perform, or what feats I can accomplish if I don't have love. If I have all of these other things but not love, I am no more valuable to the body than a clanging cymbal. Following this, Paul tells us what love is.

1 Corinthians 13:4-7 Charity suffereth long, *and* is kind; charity envieth not; charity vaunteth not itself, is not puffed up, Doth not behave itself unseemly, seeketh not her own, is not easily provoked, thinketh no evil; Rejoiceth not in iniquity, but rejoiceth in the truth; Beareth all things, believeth all things, hopeth all things, endureth all things.

You may have read these words dozens of times and each time seen areas where you dropped the ball. There may be some thoughts that we typically have about love that we do not find in this description.

Many will say very sincerely, I just don't love him/her anymore. I wish I could, but too much has happened. The thesis of that statement is that love is an emotion, a warm bubbly, positive feeling one has for a member of the opposite sex. You either have it or you don't. If you don't, there is nothing you can do about it. You simply move away and hope that you may find it with someone else someday, somewhere. Some people believe that they need to divorce their spouses because they've fallen out of love. To them, love is a feeling that is either there or it's not there. If it's there, you get married. If it's not there, you divorce. This is one of the silliest ideas I have ever heard. First of all, people don't just fall out of love. If love dwindles, it's because the marriage wasn't a priority. Love is a living thing. If you nurture it, it grows. If you neglect it, it dies. Love is not the tingly feeling. Love is a choice. It is an intentional decision. Love does not knock us down by surprise. It is something over which we have complete control. Now please don't misunderstand me about feelings. I love ecstasy and butterflies and all of the wild feelings that we typically attach to the idea of love. It is wonderful when those feelings accompany love, and they often do in the early stages. That is not where we usually run into problems. It is later on, when the feelings have dissipated, that we get into trouble. Then we have to deal with the fact that feelings are nice, but they are not love. The decisions and choices that I make about how I determine to treat another are what love is about.

I am divorced and in my second marriage. I know the word divorce very well but I am blessed that the divorce process was quick and there were no children involved. I don't want to bash my ex here so what I'm going to say is after thirteen years my ex went through a metamorphosis. She changed into one that had a spiritual hold on my every thought. I talked more about all of it in my book "The Stronghold of Jezebel". After years of torment I would not give up on the marriage until God released me. God said go and I left. Understand I've been in the prophetic ministry over twenty years. I know God's voice. When I left my eyes saw all the damage to the Body of Christ from the headship of my ex. I went through many months of tears and emotional shifts. God has truly restored my life, ministry and my second marriage is great. My wife and I just had our beautiful daughter Arianna and I know that it is truly God's blessing and forgiveness for divorce. I know without a shadow of a doubt that God hates divorce but GRACE and MERCY with a bucket of forgiveness I have been healed and set free. You can too! May you find Healing After Divorce or whatever situation your life's journey has taken you.

About the Author

Bill Vincent is no stranger to understanding the power of God. Not only has he spent over twenty years as a Minister with a strong prophetic anointing, he is now also an Apostle and Author with Revival Waves of Glory Ministries in Litchfield, IL. Along with his wife, Tabitha, he, leads a team providing apostolic oversight in all aspects of ministry, including service, personal ministry and Godly character.

Bill offers a wide range of writings and teachings from deliverance, to experiencing presence of God and developing Apostolic cutting edge Church structure. Drawing on the power of the Holy Spirit through years of experience in Revival, Spiritual Sensitivity, and deliverance ministry, Bill now focuses mainly on pursuing the Presence of God and breaking the power of the devil off of people's lives.

His books 48 and counting has since helped many people to overcome the spirits and curses of Satan. For more information or to keep up with Bill's latest releases, please visit www.revivalwavesofgloryministries.com. To contact Bill, feel free to follow him on twitter @revivalwaves.

Recommended Books

By Bill Vincent

Overcoming Obstacles

Glory: Pursuing God's Presence

Defeating the Demonic Realm

Increasing Your Prophetic Gift

Increasing Your Anointing

Keys to Receiving Your Miracle

The Supernatural Realm

Waves of Revival

Increase of Revelation and Restoration

The Resurrection Power of God

Discerning Your Call of God

Apostolic Breakthrough

Glory: Increasing God's Presence

Love is Waiting – Don't Let Love Pass You By

The Healing Power of God

Glory: Expanding God's Presence

Receiving Personal Prophecy

Signs and Wonders

Signs and Wonders Revelations

Children Stories

The Rapture

The Secret Place of God's Power

Building a Prototype Church

Breakthrough of Spiritual Strongholds

Glory: Revival Presence of God

Overcoming the Power of Lust

Glory: Kingdom Presence of God

Transitioning Into a Prototype Church

The Stronghold of Jezebel

Healing After Divorce

A Closer Relationship With God

Cover Up and Save Yourself

Desperate for God's Presence

The War for Spiritual Battles

Spiritual Leadership

Global Warning

There Are Millions of Churches

Destroying the Jezebel Spirit

Awakening of Miracles

Deception and Consequences Revealed

Are You a Follower of Christ

Don't Let the Enemy Steal from You!

A Godly Shaking

The Unsearchable Riches of Christ

Heaven's Court System

Satan's Open Doors

Armed for Battle

The Wrestler

Spiritual Warfare: Complete Collection

Growing In the Prophetic

The Prototype Church: Complete Edition

Faith

The Rapture

To Order:

Email:

rwgcontact@yahoo.com

Web Site:

www.revivalwavesofgloryministries.com

Mail Order:

Revival Waves of Glory

PO Box 596

Litchfield, IL 62056

Shipping $5.00

If you mail an order and pay by check, make check out to Revival Waves of Glory.

Most books are in multiple formats such as Hardcover, Soft-Cover, Ebook (such as Kindle & Nook), and Audio Books.

SD - #0011 - 070726 - C0 - 216/138/9 - PB - 9780692648681 - Gloss Lamination